Meet You at the Top
A Journal of Love and Faith

Martha Langford Derrick

"For I have learned, in whatsoever state I am, therewith to be content."
"I can do all things through Christ which strengthens me."
Apostle Paul – Philippians 4:11 and 13

"A merry heart doeth good like a medicine" – Proverbs 17:22

Published by
Evening Post Books
Charleston, South Carolina

Copyright © 2024 Martha Langford Derrick
All rights reserved.
First edition

Author: Martha Langford Derrick
Editor: Robert Stockton
Designer: Gill Guerry

Front cover photograph: Martha and Fletcher Derrick on their 50th wedding anniversary, 2006.

Back cover photograph: All the grandchildren - six boys and one girl.

First printing 2024
Printed in the United States of America

A CIP catalog record for this book has been applied
for from the Library of Congress.

ISBN: 978-1-929647-96-5

DEDICATION

This book is lovingly dedicated to my children,

grandchildren, and great grandchildren.

Martha (Mottie) Sansbury Derrick Wieters,

Fletcher Carl Derrick III, MD

Grandchildren: Eliza Langford Rodrigue McElwee MD

Ronald Rex Rodrigue, Jr.

Derrick August Wieters

Owen Anderson Wieters

Heyward Fletcher Derrick

Crosson Bradford Derrick

Stuart Langford Derrick

Gabriella Sakzenian O'Quinn

Louise Derrick McElwee

Katherine Auld McElwee

ACKNOWLEDGMENTS

I wish to thank the following people who helped me along the way: Robert P. Stockton, Editor (friend for many years), Lucy Royal and Ted McDermoot who were the "early" typists (Lucy, the Care Navigator for Bishop Gadsden, did many things for me and offered much encouragement – we became good friends), Lynn Richmond, who worked with me to help keep this project going – giving much excellent advice and always there for me, and last, but not least, my daughter Martha (Mottie) Wieters and my son, Carl Derrick, without whose support I could not have written this – they lived so much of this, and it is their story, also.

How fortunate I am to have cousins that were interested in my plans and gave much help and information along the way –

Langford cousins (living)
    Jane Sizemore Tutterow
    Sally Fe Sizemore
    Jimmy Langford Sizemore

Sansbury cousins (living)
    Harriett Wade McElveen
    Kathleen (Kathy) Wade
    Peggy Wade Platt

My first cousin - Dora Sansbury Schwartz - died before this book was published. Through the years, she did exhaustive research on the Sansbury family. I am indebted to her for her excellent work, and she lives in a part of this book.

CONTENTS

MY LIFE'S DEDICATION
– Martha Langford Derrick

I have a BS degree in Business Education and a minor in history from Coker College. I went there because that is where my mother and all my aunts studied. I received a scholarship, and I typed for the English Department. My father insisted that I get a business degree. He was very ill when I went to college, and I didn't know how long I could stay. But my love was history – since the fourth grade when my teachers started talking about continents, rivers, peninsulas, etc. I enjoyed and loved college, and graduated with honors: Sophiades Honor Society, Who's Who in American Colleges and Universitys, President of the Christian Association, and Editor of the college newspaper. My husband Fletcher came to medical school after his third year at Clemson. He had missed all his electives in art, history, and religion, so I had a wonderful time teaching him, and he was an extremely eager student.

It was settled that I teach school in the Charleston County school system. I could be home more with Fletcher than if I had an executive position. So, I taught typing and shorthand during the school year and world history during the summer. The Saturdays Fletcher was at the hospital I modeled clothes for a department store.

In the summer world history class, I had everybody in Charleston County who failed that subject during the year, mostly boys. They could not care less about history; and the principal told me I was to teach only a few points, and they would all pass. I had fun with it. I taught people and places. They will never forget Henry VIII and his six wives – divorced, beheaded, died, divorced, beheaded, out-lived him. No one will ever forget Marie Antoinette and the loss of her head. One time in France I went to the Temple Prison where she was held. I then walked the way of a small, wheeled open cart (tumbrel) in which she sat with hands tied behind her back, grey hair cropped, to the Place de la Concorde where the guillotine stood. Also, I liked to teach battles, so Napoleon became a favorite, along with Caesar and Rommel and many others with as much of history as possible. I made it fun, and interesting and they seemed to enjoy it.

The only thing I didn't like was leaving my three-year-old daughter when I taught. I wish I could do it all over again. I always found time to be active in my church – teaching adult Sunday school and working as a deacon and elder.

My main dedication was to Fletcher and his career. A happy wonderful marriage was so inspiring and much more important than anything else I could have done.

PERSONAL HISTORY

I was born on November 22, 1934, in an apartment on South Broughton Street in Orangeburg, SC. I was to be an only child, to be named Lois (after my mother) and Martha (after her best friend). We lived there for a little while and then moved soon to the St. Joseph Hotel as this was during the Depression, and jobs were scarce. This move was to bring me great joy for all my life. My parents made friends with another couple – Mary and Lee Wyndham. They never had any children and we loved each other, and I was like their child. So I really had two sets of parents. They lived in Columbia, and I spent several weeks with them every summer. My father had to call and make me come home. They showed me great attention and affection. I called them Manie and Poppa Lee. After Poppa Lee died, Manie came to Germany and spent some time with us. She died several years ago holding my hand and telling me she loved me more than anyone in the world. She and her husband brought additional happiness and love into my world already filled with an abundance from my parents.

When I was about three years old, we moved to a house on Elliott Street. Surrounded by Wannamakers, I did not lack for playmates. Those were happy years for me. I keep in touch with the last one left – Dr. Braxton Wannamaker. He and Evelyn Wannamaker Richards are still a part of my life.

About the age of ten we moved across town to the last house on Carolina Avenue, going toward the Edisto River. I was very lonely there but spent my time babysitting and playing the piano. Mrs. Angie McMichael was my teacher. I had no real talent but loved to play. Miss Angie had a Saturday morning music club in which we studied the lives of the composers. There were about four boys and myself in these sessions which meant a great deal to me.

I spent a lot of time just walking down by the river, picking blackberries, and pretending I was Sacagawea, the Indian woman who went with Lewis and Clark on their expedition to the West.

Books have always been important to me. When we lived on Elliott Street, the city library was just several blocks away. My mother and I would walk there every week. She would allow me only three books a week and that was not nearly enough. *The Nancy Drew Mystery Stories* were a favorite. Today I read nearly three books a week, mostly non-fiction.

When I was in the ninth grade, I was chosen to be the manager of the girls' basketball team. I had the responsibility of keeping the score and helping with oranges and chocolate at halftime. I loved high school and the teachers, many great ones. I did have some things to overcome, but my faith in God really helped me. At the age of sixteen, I realized how important God is and the First Baptist Church was to me. I knew what kind of person I wanted to be and what I wanted out of life. I prayed God would send me someone who would share my dreams.

That came to be true in college. The Coker girls and the cadets at Clemson had deputation teams with each other for weekends. It was at Clemson that I first saw Fletcher Derrick. He came over to me and asked if I was from Orangeburg and if I knew somebody. He then walked away. I was puzzled. He then dated many of my friends. One summer day in 1955, he wrote me and asked me to help with a summer revival in Parksville, SC, near Augusta. He had a friend (a Furman ministerial student who would preach) and Fletcher would lead the music. He wanted me to play the piano and organ. I was delighted. That was just what I liked to do.

Well – something happened that neither of us planned. In that week we were constantly together and fell in love! We both knew it was the real thing. While Fletcher was singing one night and I was playing the organ, I looked up at him and my heart did a flip. It was real! All of this created quite a bit of trouble because both of us were dating other people. Things slowly worked out, and we were married about a year later. I asked Fletcher, "why - of all the girls you dated - did you choose to marry me?" He replied, "I love you very much - and besides - you have depth." I was very pleased. I taught school while he finished medical school and a residency and then we started life's journey together. We had a wonderful love affair until Fletcher's death in 2020 – sixty-four years. He died with my arms around him. God did answer my prayer.

THE EDISTO RIVER

Growing up in Orangeburg, the Edisto River was a very important part of my life. When I was young, I would beg my mother to take me swimming every day. There was no public swimming pool in the city. The river made a lovely turn in Orangeburg, which made a great swimming place. The mothers would sit on a bench under the cypress trees and watch us carefully.

The river is one of the longest free-flowing black waters which run in North America. It rises from springs just south of the Piedmont Falls – near the towns of Saluda and Edgefield. My husband always liked to say, the Edisto began in the woods and fields behind his home in Johnston. It seems that Fletcher was right; the Edisto River that flows through Orangeburg is technically the North Fork. The South Fork has its beginnings in Johnston, SC. Along the way, it passes near Denmark and Bamberg, SC. The South Fork and North Fork merge about 5 miles below Branchville to form the Edisto River.

The river flows over 250 meandering miles from its source to the Atlantic Ocean. It is the longest and largest river system completely contained by the borders of South Carolina. Its name comes from the Edisto subtribe of the Cusabo Indians.

The river flows throughout its entire length through bottom swampland. During the rainy season its basin increases to over a mile or more in total width. The lower Edisto, along with the Ashepoo and Combahee rivers, form the ACE Basin. A major tributary is Four Holes swamp, which is unique in that it has no single defined channel, but rather a network of braided channels.

"Edisto Riverkeeper"

"The Edisto Riverkeeper is a non-profit 501(c)(3) organization working to ensure equal access to drinkable, fishable, and swimmable water in the Edisto River basin and its surrounding aquifers and tributaries. As one of over 330 members to the Waterkeeper Alliance, Edisto Riverkeeper seeks to encourage balanced usage of the basin's water resources for residents, industry, and municipalities to utilize and enjoy through education, advocacy, and accountability."

"Friends of the Edisto"

"Friends of the Edisto, Inc." –FRED–, a non-profit organization, was established in 1998 to facilitate conservation of natural resources and to encourage and support sustainable economic development within the Edisto River Basin in South Carolina."

"Edisto River Canoe and Kayak Trail"

"Edisto River Canoe and Kayak Trail" –EREK– is a group of volunteers committed to the preservation of the Edisto River, educating people on safe paddling, and emphasizing the enjoyment of paddling. All instructors are American Canoe Association certified."

The river provides much enjoyment around Orangeburg. My father would not go near it; he said it was the coldest water anywhere and too swift a current. (It is fed by an artesian well that made the water feel cool and refreshing.) I think some people don't like it because of the black water (caused by tannic acid from the cypress trees in the swamp). When we came from living in Germany, our daughter was two years old and did not know her colors. The first day we were at home, my parents drove her down to the river. She said, "It's a chocolate river!"

That chocolate river could be scary at times. We swam around the shore and dared to swim to the bridge. There was a rope under the bridge. If you did not catch it, you floated into the dangerous territory. I remember the first time I did it, I was really scared. That rope felt so good in my hands. There was always a group of boys – West, Tom, Bert, and others who had a giant rope around a tree – they would swing and then they would drop into the water - and this provided good watching.

And – oh, what fun the teenagers had in the summertime in and around the lovely building the city provided with a small restaurant and music to dance to on the patio.

I will never forget the house parties at Edisto Beach. That is where Orangeburg people went to the beach. Yes, the river gave us many memories.

The Edisto Memorial Gardens were a dream of many in Orangeburg in 1927. After receiving the commitment from City Council to establish these gardens, a Mr. Sifly turned to Mrs. Leila B. Jervey, an Orangeburg florist, for guidance. She in turn contacted Mr. Frederick (Fritz) Aichele, a professional nurseryman, from North Charleston.

When Mr. Aichele arrived in Orangeburg to evaluate the site for these future gardens, to obtain the information needed to create a design, the area was so boggy he had to go to Orangeburg's fire station to borrow some fireman's boots to be able to do so. After surveying the site, he and Mrs. Jervey went back to the floral shop where he proceeded to draw the plans for Orangeburg's new gardens. He had to do so on the back of a piece of cardboard from a flower carton, as no large size paper was available. What an interesting beginning for what are now some of the most beautiful gardens in all of South Carolina.

Since very few plant nurseries were around in those days, Mr. Aichele's firm was also hired to supply and install these initial plantings of azaleas. Prior to doing so, topsoil had to be hauled in to eliminate the wetness as well as provide adequate nutrients for these new shrubs.

Mrs. Jervey's son Jimmy, then an eager teenager, was among those who unloaded the first deliveries of topsoil. He later would stake out locations for all the plants from Mr. Aichele's landscape design.

The first azaleas were shipped up to Orangeburg on a railroad boxcar. Afterwards, Mr. Aichele's crew planted these azaleas to create the beginning of what is now Orangeburg's legacy, our very beautiful Edisto Memorial Gardens.

Ironically, about fifteen years later, Mr. Aichele's daughter moved to Orangeburg to live upon her marriage as Mrs. Cliff (Ruth) Morgan.

It's a small world. Laura Aichele Wilson - VP of Marketing at Bishop Gadsden - is the granddaughter of Frederick Aichele. Her cousins here in Charleston are now some of my best friends - Dale and Marty Murray. Dale and I worked together at the Historic Charleston Foundation for many years. I - and my family - will all be indebted to Mr. Aichele who created such beauty for us to enjoy.

Dr. Gene Atkinson provided me with much of the information in this story. I am very grateful to him for his interesting knowledge.

Today, over 600,000 visitors come every year from all fifty states as well as several foreign countries. It is nestled among the tall, stately cypress trees along the Edisto River. It is open 365 days a year with no admission charge. Around 1951, a rose garden of 2,500 roses was established. A water wheel, Hisada gardens, and many azaleas were added to the romantic gardens. My mother's favorites were over 90 beautiful Yoshino cherry trees, gifts from the people of Orangeburg. Today, the entire area encompassing Edisto Memorial Gardens and its outlying areas is over 2,000 acres.

"May a Spark of the Beauty
Beholden to You Here at Edisto Gardens,
Kindle Within You a Flame of Desire
To Go Forth and Make More Beautiful
This Great Land of Ours,
Wherever Your Lot Is Cast."

– Andrew C. Dibble, Circa 1948

LIVING WITH A BULLY

"Into every life some rain must fall." Well, I had a hurricane come into my life. Strange things started to happen to me in the eighth and ninth grades. A "friend" started being very mean to me. I did not understand; I had never done anything to her.

1. I had warts all over my hands, especially on top of my hands and around the cuticles. I was so ashamed. The Bully said to me, "If I was a boy, I would not want to hold hands with you." That hurt! Finally, my parents took me to Columbia to a specialist and he used spray, surgery and heat to make them all disappear.

2. Vocabulary has never been my "thing." When I was young and sick, I always read the encyclopedia. I loved learning about places and people but never paid much attention to the words. One day in English class, we were studying vocabulary. The teacher asked me to define the word *meager*. I did not know the word. So, the teacher asked the person behind me the same question. That person happened to be the Bully and she said, "Martha has a meager amount of brains." I was so embarrassed – but I never forgot the word meager.

3. Our class voted for a girl to have an honor I really wanted. They chose me. The Bully went to the person working with the honor and persuaded her to delete my name and name someone else. I never understood that, but what could I do without causing a scene?

4. I was dating a very nice, popular boy. The Bully said to me, "The other boys don't like him."

5. She organized the SUS Club (Stuck Up Sisters). I was horrified and thought it so silly – but I joined. All of my friends were members. I constantly tried to disband the club and every time she came at me with more vengeance. I was furious!

I never told anybody any of this, including my parents. Then one day I went to visit a classmate in another state. She immediately started telling me all the things the Bully had done to her, some of which could have led to her alcoholism in later life. She was dating one of the nicest and smartest boys in our class. The Bully said to her, "The only reason you got a part in the Senior Class play is because you never had any other honor." (The Bully did not get a part in the play.)

I was so disturbed about that. Could it be that I was not the only one she bullied? Could it really be a pattern of behavior? What was the Bully facing in her life that caused her to have such behavior? I began to see her in a different light. She must have been so unhappy with such negative behavior. I really found forgiveness for her for all she had done to me. I try to pray for her every night that she might realize what unhappiness she caused and maybe try to make amends.

I have managed to have a wonderful life in spite of all of this. Sometimes it has been hard.

MARTIN LUTHER AND JOHN CALVIN

It was my inspiration to visit the places associated with Luther and Calvin. We rented a car in Berlin and drove to Wittenberg, which was in East Germany and not available to visit until recent years. Luther protested the sale of indulgences and made his mark with the 95 Theses, which he posted on the door of the castle church at Wittenberg. The original door is not there but I stood in that place and remembered all the things he did for me with those Theses and other thoughts: the Bible is the only infallible source of religious authority; the priesthood of the believer; salvation is a free gift of God received only by true repentance and faith in Jesus as the Messiah. There was so much he added to my faith, and I am very grateful for his courage and fortitude – what a great day!

I went on a Huguenot tour of France and saw the home of John Calvin in that country. However, for his safety he spent most of his life in Switzerland, especially in Geneva. Fletcher had a cousin who was an Ambassador in Geneva and invited us as house guests. What a thrill it was to stand behind Calvin's pulpit and sit in his chair. After the Revocation of the Edict of Nantes in 1685, many Huguenots (Protestants following the teachings of Calvin) were killed and more than 250,000 left France. My ancestors were among them. Calvin was a major force in the spread of Reformed Theology. He is famous for his teachings and writings. He was a central developer of the system of Christian theology called Calvinism or Reformed Theology.

Luther and Calvin were directly responsible for the way I use my faith every day. Calvin knew the benefits of business and was instrumental in founding and developing the silk industry in Geneva by which Genevans reaped monetary benefits. He touched many lives in "new" ways of thinking. I am so glad whenever I learn some other "pearl of wisdom" he left for me. His and Luther's voluminous publications exert a lasting influence over Christianity and Western history.

MY ENGLISH ANCESTORS

My English ancestors are Sansbury memories. The first Sansbury arrived in Darlington County, South Carolina, around 1740. Daniel Sansbury is the first we have record of. He fought with General Francis Marion during the Revolutionary War. Francis Marion was known as the Swamp Fox. He and his men wore the colors of the swamps of the Pee Dee and Santee rivers; they knew how to live there.

There were more Revolutionary battles fought in South Carolina than in any other state. Francis Marion and other Southern leaders kept the British so tangled up down here and so enabled Washington and other leaders in the North to win victories there. The first decisive battle of the war was at Fort Moultrie in Charleston Harbor June 28, 1776, in which we won mainly because the fort was made of palmetto logs which resisted the British cannon balls. A courier was hurriedly sent to Philadelphia where the Continental Congress was meeting to prove that maybe the British could be defeated. They signed the Declaration of Independence days later. There were four signers from South Carolina. One of these was Thomas Heyward, Jr., the ancestor of some of my grandsons, one of whose name is Heyward Fletcher Derrick.

The Sansburys probably came from England by way of Virginia. It is now one of the most prominent names in England. The Sansburys own the largest market business in England where you see many of their signs and trucks. The Sansburys married into the Hatchell, Anderson, Hill, Miles and Stokes families. There was an Uncle Sumter whom I assume was my grandfather's brother. I think it is unusual and important that my grandfather had a cousin named Culpepper Hill. Culpepper is a name found mostly in Virginia. Many English families came to South Carolina from Virginia.

Now I would like to talk about the Sansbury home. I only saw the home in the country once. It was a sprawling one-storied wooden house with porches all around. The thing my mother, Lois, remembered most about that house was when my grandmother (Ga-Ga) was taking care of her, and her long skirt caught on fire. Ga-Ga wrapped herself in a rug and rolled on the floor to put the fire out. She was left with many burns on her body, but she saved lives and the house.

My grandfather evidently became more prosperous, and they moved to the large Victorian (Queen Anne style) on Byrd Street in Timmonsville around 1910. He paid $48,000 in cash. That home was magic to me; my fondest childhood memories were spent there. I always spent several weeks in the summer there where tobacco season was exciting in the town.

The railroad ran straight from Orangeburg to Florence, with a Timmonsville stop on the way. I must have been about nine years old when my parents first put me on the train to get off in Timmonsville. I was always terrified that I wouldn't get off in the right place.

Of course, we all went to Timmonsville for holidays. The house was quite large: two parlors, five bedrooms, a large dining room, and the family was so proud to live in the first home in Florence County to have two inside bathrooms. The house had parquet floors. There were nine fireplaces; the formal ones were "catty-cornered" – very typical of a house built at that time. There was a large curving stairway to the right as you entered the home, with little benches that opened underneath the stairway. I played there under the stairs all the time.

The stairs curved right up to the second floor. Three bedrooms were used; the front left bedroom was the guest room. It had two double beds and a curtain in the corner as a closet. This is where I slept unless I was in Ga-Ga's room. My favorite memory in this room was waking up in the morning and Tom (Lou's husband) was making a crackling fire because the house had no central heat.

Another bedroom was not used at all, and it was spooky. Old clothes were scattered around, open trunks with clothes everywhere. There were even birds in and out of broken windowpanes. My cousin Tom said he and Austin played there and found a lot of Confederate money. What happened to it? I wondered.

There was a large hall. My cousin Grady Jr. and I put a pallet in the middle to take our afternoon rest. In the back was a large sleeping porch. There were about three double beds there. There was a small back stairway that was meant to be used only by servants. It was very narrow and steep.

The lot next door had been our tennis court in the early days. There was much laughing and teasing on the front porch every afternoon. The neighbors must have wondered what was going on. There was a big stone carriage block at the front walk to get in and out of a carriage or to get on and off a horse.

The present owners removed that and the one at the back door.

Ga-Ga always sat at the head of the table. She had the habit of dunking her toast in her coffee. There was always a roaring fire in the dining room. Lou ordered the groceries for the day from the telephone right under the back stairways. It was a black telephone that you held one part to your ear and talked into the other part. Groceries were delivered every day and always at the back door. Black people never came to the front door – that "unwritten rule" would remain until the 1960s.

My grandmother, Ga-Ga – Minnie Anderson Sansbury – was reared near Darlington and Timmonsville and near the Lake Swamp Baptist Church. She was the warmest person I have ever known, and I wanted to be just like her. She had a sister, Amanda; I remember visiting her once. Ga-Ga had bad arthritis and she never went out of the house except to water the plants on the porch and rake magnolia leaves. She had long grey hair that I often combed and brushed for her. I usually slept in the same room as she, in the other double bed. The room was warm because the family sitting room next door had a coal fired stove. We would talk late into the night.

My grandfather James Baxter Sansbury was reared in the same vicinity as Ga-Ga. His mother was Elizabeth Hill. He taught school at some point in his life. He had a commissary on his land where the sharecroppers would get their food every Saturday. He was a pillar of the church in Timmonsville and the church treasurer for many years.

He, being such a strict Baptist deacon, the family was surprised one day when he told this story. "Minnie is always late to come to bed. She roams around the house until after midnight. So, the next time I get married, I am most definitely going to sleep with her first. Nothing would go on in bed; I just want to know what time she comes to sleep! If it is after midnight, I would forget the relationship."

I once saw tears come into my Uncle Lemont's eyes when he spoke of his father. He must have been a great man.

This is what I have always been told. Our grandfather was the President of the bank when the Depression came. He also had many plantations, and they were very profitable. In those days it was legal to put everything in your wife's name without waiting a length of time. Therefore, my grandfather wouldn't have been liable for anything. However, my grandfather called his children in and told them he couldn't morally do that. He wouldn't let all the farmers with money in his bank lose everything they had. He was going to see that was not done. He would save all their land for them although it would take all he had to do it. He thought that was the moral thing to do. He did it and was left with almost nothing. Uncle Lemont bought the house so my family would have a place to live.

I remember going to see him in the hospital after a train wreck. Everybody thought he was all right, but he had internal injuries that weren't known for several days. The family was eating dinner when the doctor – probably Dr. Simmons – came up the walk and told them that he had died. I remember pictures of his grave absolutely covered with flowers. His death was a great loss to the community. He was a man of much integrity.

My grandfather was the finest of men. He loved to ride over his land on a black horse named Sampson. I do remember sitting in his lap at one time. That is all I know about him.

My mother, Lois Sansbury, was reared in the country and attended Coker College at a very early age. She was so smart that she finished college at age eighteen. Ga-Ga said, "We should always do what Lois says; it is the best." Lois was one the others should emulate. She was a favorite of my grandfather. She was reared in luxury. She always wore a bonnet when she went outside. Years later when we went to the beach, we never went until 5:00 p.m., but still she had many skin cancers on her face. Let a dermatologist figure that out! She always wore a hat to church, and I buried her in a pink hat.

In Orangeburg she met my father, James Crosson Langford, who was called Red because he had red hair. He had finished The Citadel and studied civil engineering. He worked for the state highway department. The Depression came and times were hard, but my mother didn't teach school again until I left for college.

My father had stomach ulcers; he stayed in bed a great deal of time, drinking only cream. At that time ulcers were thought to be caused by anxiety and spicy foods, so he was very careful about what he ate. Today all we do is give an antibiotic, and the ulcers are gone. But he went through several operations and many days in bed. It was very, very sad.

My mother had a lot to endure and many uncertain times. However, she was very talented and made all my clothes. I never had a bought dress until I was thirteen. Sewing and bridge were her hobbies. She had never been in a kitchen until she married, but she came to be an excellent cook.

I was named for Martha Thurmond, Senator Strom Thurmond's sister, with whom my mother had roomed while teaching, and who introduced my mother and father. Big Martha, as I called her, married Dr. Walter Bishop in Greenwood. She was always so kind to me and gave me a piece of silver every birthday.

I went to Coker College – had no choice. I married Fletcher Carl Derrick Jr., when he was in medical school. We had two children: Martha Sansbury Derrick and Fletcher Carl Derrick, III.

Daughter Martha, known as Mottie, married Paul Wieters, who was the City of Charleston recreation director and (after a first retirement) is now the Wellness Coordinator for Charleston. Mottie is an English teacher at West Ashley High School. At the time they were married, Mottie had two children, Eliza Langford Rodrigue and Ronald Rex Rodrigue, Jr. Paul and Mottie added Derrick August Wieters and Owen Anderson Wieters to their family. Owen has been diagnosed with Dravet Syndrome, which is a seizure disorder requiring constant care; Paul has said that Owen is the joy of his life. Paul's family came over from Germany about 1870, and they were all active members of St. Matthew's Lutheran Church where they now worship.

Son Carl became a doctor. He went to Hampden-Sidney College in Virginia and the Medical University of South Carolina, in Charleston. He practices internal medicine in Beaufort, South Carolina. He has three children; Heyward Fletcher Derrick, Crosson (my father's middle name) Bradford Derrick, and Stuart Langford Derrick. Crosson was a twin, and we lost his little brother William at birth. Carl is married now to a Brazilian ballerina, who has a daughter named Gabriella (Carl loves having a girl in his family). How about three in college at the same time! Melissa formed the Derrick Ballet Conservatory and enhances the town of Beaufort with her exquisite performances each year.

As a Clemson University trustee, Fletcher presented Heyward his diploma with a hug and a kiss, and the audience clapped. At that time Fletcher was dying and several other trustees helped him with the diploma. Fletcher kept saying, "One day in a lifetime."

Mother's brothers Lemont and Jack, and my father loved to hunt birds; they had such a good time doing it. We had a huge back porch, and they would come in laughing, having much fun with many birds and I would help pick them, and we had them the next morning with grits. It was exciting when they would go hunting. Poppa had a black friend, Moise, and they hunted on his land. Mrs. Moise always prepared the dinner for them. There was much merriment and teasing.

Mother's sister Lillian's middle name was Floride. I called her Ninny. She and her husband, Grady Wade, moved into the house and ran it for my grandmother. I loved her dearly, and she was so special to me. She had an older son, Grady Jr., and every time he went out at night he would come in and tell my grandmother goodnight. I slept in the other bed in her room and thought it was so exciting that he would do that every night. He died a premature death of a stroke at age fifty-two. Lillian always had the children in Timmonsville over to our house when I was there, and we would sit around the dining room table and have grape juice and graham crackers. There wasn't much said because we didn't know each other. Lillian had a happy yet sad life. Arnold was her daughter, and we were close.

Jack had twins, Dora and Austin. It happened that twins ran every other generation in our family. My son had twins. Ga-Ga had a twin brother and sister who died at birth.

Then there was Mother's sister Edith. She was in the train wreck in which my grandfather was fatally injured. She never was the same again and lived a very unfortunate life.

Mother's sister Crystal and her husband Bill were the light of my life. They were always in my life. I can't imagine how my life would have been without them. They had a son named Tom who has recently passed away and was the only first cousin I had left on the Sansbury side. Bill was a Catholic and at that time their marriage was called a mixed marriage, but everyone loved Bill and approved of him. Crystal and Bill came to Timmonsville when Tommy was about three months old. For the first time I saw friction between Ga-Ga and Lillian when they both wanted to hold him first.

I end with Lou. Lou was the maid and the cook, and she really ran the house. She was big and fat like the character Mammy in *Gone with the Wind*. She cooked on a wood stove. She could make the best biscuits and pineapple cake. I spent much time in the kitchen with her. She used to tease me about eating so much. She had a daughter named Blue. Her husband was Tom and he sort of acted as a chauffeur or butler. I don't know what happened to Lou.

The big house burned, and Lillian just slowly died.

Ga-Ga's hands were crippled with arthritis. But when I was staying there, she always wanted help in writing letters to her children. She always said, "Never write a letter without a funny." That I have never forgotten.

What I have written is what I have witnessed and continually heard from my parents. I haven't included anything from anybody else.

So, this is the story about the aristocracy of a small town in South Carolina during and after the Depression.

MY GERMAN ANCESTRY
Compiled by Fred Swygert

My paternal grandfather, James David Langford, (of English and French Huguenot ancestry) was widowed and left with four children. Then arrived my grandmother, who was pure German. Her name was Lilla Swygert. She was hardworking, tough and a fighter. She had to be all those things because her life was very hard. Our family has always said, "never underestimate a Swygert-Langford woman." She came from a small town in Germany called Erpfingen.

Many of Martin Luther's followers came under considerable religious persecution because of their beliefs. They came from Germany, Holland, Switzerland and beyond and shared a common view of the religion. Many came to a region called the Palatinate, of which Heidelberg was then the capital. During the Reformation the Palatinate became the foremost Calvinistic region in Germany.

There were wars being fought based on politics and religious hatred as armies sought to crush the religious freedom of a politically divided Protestantism.

While the land of the Palatinate was good for its inhabitants (many of whom were farmers, vineyard operators, etc.), its location was unfortunately subject to invasion by the armies of Britain, France, and Germany. The winter of 1708 was particularly severe, and they lost many vineyards.

A great number were going to leave this area in the spring of 1709. About 7,000 Palatinates sailed down the Rhine on the way to America.

There were many reasons for this immigration: obsessive taxation, religious bickering and wanting better and more land. Then they heard about the English colonies in America and the favorable attitude of the British government for settlement in the colonies there.

In 1710, three large groups sailed from the Palatinate; one came to Carolina. They left a life that was dull, monotonous, restrictive, uncertain, and seemingly hopeless. They came for freedom in all endeavors. The crossing usually took about five weeks.

About this time the eight Lord Proprietors of Carolina, named by Charles II, advertised in the Palatinate for "strong men of the soil" to come to Carolina – promising free passage and fifty acres. Many came and settled around the rivers Broad, Saluda, Congaree, and Santee, in the vicinity of Lexington, Columbia, Leesville, etc. The purpose of their being there was to act as a buffer between the Indian tribes and Charleston and its surrounding plantations. This area was called Dutch Fork or really Deutsch Fork.

There were also French Huguenots with them, and they settled on the Savannah River in Carolina and called the town Purrysburg. My family probably was from both groups who settled there. In just three years there were a hundred houses and about 156 settlers in Purrysburg. They represented every skilled craft and profession and practically all were educated. They raised silkworms, grapes, olives and indigo.

The Purrysburg settlement didn't survive the new great railroad passing it. There is some history showing that Sherman and his men took drastic toll on their way to Columbia.

Some of the Germans became an important factor in the history of the city of Charleston with names such as Bachman, Horlbeck, Brandt, Mappus, Siegling and Hanckel. My son-in-law's forbearers – the Wieters, came around 1870 and were always devoted to St. Matthews Lutheran Church. Paul Wieters was president of the congregation in 2021. These people helped make Charleston the most cosmopolitan city in the new world in the 18th century.

My husband's family was in this group. The name Dietrich was changed to Derrick. The Derrick name belonged to many doctors and Lutheran ministers. When they couldn't farm anymore, they chose mostly these two professions.

In 1735 these were the two types of settlers that the king wanted to populate the back country and cut from the wilderness a thriving economy. This they did in abundance.

The forest was full of wild game and the rivers furnished an abundance of fish and oysters. Corn and its use as a meal and mush were adopted from Indians, and is use with venison and other meats furnished the settlers with their main foods. A settler could come from his own doorway and shoot enough game for his table.

Mr. Hoy Caughman, in his book "Cedar Grove Lutheran Church 1852-2002" described the Germans that settled the Dutch Fork area of South Carolina as having integrity, love of freedom, and a courage that moved them to dare and to die rather than to surrender their principles.

My paternal grandparents, the Langfords, were cousins. Grandmother Lilla always called my grandfather Cousin Jimmy. My mother thought him "unusual" the first time she went to the home. He wore his hat to eat at the table and took it off to say the blessing. He died at age sixty-nine and the state newspaper printed an account of his death and called him a member of a "large and highly respected family." He had led a very active, energetic, unselfish, and exemplary life. He was a farmer and stock raiser. The *State* newspaper said he was one of the most highly regarded and honored citizens.

Tragedy struck my grandmother again when the Depression came and the bank in Columbia foreclosed and took everything she had. Everything was mortgaged and anything on the premises "house, furniture, crops" was taken. The grandfather clock was hidden under straw in a barn. She had nothing but nine children to rear. She and her sister Aunt Minnie started operating a restaurant where she cooked German cuisine. How she found a table and chairs for that restaurant I don't know. She was able to look after the children but unable to give them a college education. She reared wonderful children who loved her dearly.

My father managed to get a college education in a strange way. All his friends went to the Citadel, and that was his dream. He worked one year in the coffin factory in Leesville and got a down payment. He walked into the Citadel with one pair of pants wrapped in a newspaper and a sack of pears. He sent himself to the Citadel playing poker.

When Fletcher was in Germany, he paid a call on the Colonel at the hospital; the Colonel was from Charleston and had been in Poppa's class at the Citadel. When Fletcher asked, "did you know Red Langford?" he said, "best damn poker player there ever was!" The Colonel asked how did you know him? Fletcher said, "I married his daughter" (lots of laughter).

During World War II Poppa was 4F because of some physical ailments. We went to Columbia about every other month for Poppa to have a physical. He wanted to go in the army so badly. They always turned him down. During 1940-1945, he was a block warden on Elliott Street, and I walked along with him at night to be sure people had no lights. There was fear of Nazi submarines and bombers. He listened to the radio news of the war and played cards with me every night. He taught me how to finesse and to take a chance. Today duplicate bridge is my hobby, and I love to win. I could play every day and never be bored.

My father left the Citadel with his diploma and never played poker for money again. He had a successful career as a civil engineer, building most of I-26 from Charleston to Columbia and many other South Carolina roads.

Most people called him Red. He had curly red hair and Lilla did not cut it until he went to school. The family called him "Dolly."

EMANUEL ZEDDO SWYGERT

Emanuel Zeddo Swygert was born in the 1800s near Hollow Creek. (The next section of this book will have an article about Sherman and his army on Hollow Creek.) His father was Christian Swygert who came from Dutch Fork and settled six miles north of Leesville.

According to the 1860 census, Emanuel Zeddo Swygert owned property worth $3,000 and personal property worth $6,740. A historian of Dutch Fork said, "A man thirty-seven years old with that kind of property in that day was wealthy." He was one of the four elders who helped organize Cedar Grove Lutheran Church, established in 1852 and still a strong church today. The property on which the church was built belonged to him.

Swygert was one of the first men to join the Confederate army as a lieutenant. He was killed in action at Hilton Head during the storming of Fort Walker on November 7, 1861. His body was never found. A marker was put in the Cedar Grove cemetery in his honor.

His descendants are numerous in the Cedar Grove, Ridge Road, Batesburg, and Leesville areas. Christian was Zeddo's father – he was Lilla's Grandfather – Enoch was Lilla's father. His daughter was Lilla Swygert Langford, and her granddaughter is Martha Langford Derrick. I have two children, seven grandchildren and two great-granddaughters. I have four grandchildren with the Langford name. I live in Charleston. I was married to Dr. Fletcher Derrick who died in March of 2020.

Johannes and Christian arrived in Charleston November 1754 on board the snow class ship "Priscilla" with Captain Cattaman as ship's captain. That month they were granted 200 acres in the Fork of the Broad and Saluda rivers by the King of England.

THE REVEREND LUTHER LEGARE SWYGERT
An Autobiography

Luther Legare Swygert, son of Yoder J. and Lula Oxner Swygert, known as Legare, was born near Leesville, S.C., on August 31, 1905. He grew up in the Cedar Grover community, and attended the local country schools, completing the elementary grades. He received his high school education at the Batesburg-Leesville High School, graduating with the class of 1927. That Fall he entered Newberry College, graduating with the A.B. Degree on June 9, 1931. In the Fall of 1931, he entered the Southern Lutheran Theological Seminary, Columbia, S.C. and finished from that institution with the B.D. Degree May 17, 1934.

On May 24, 1934, he was married to Louise Addy, of the Cedar Grove community. The marriage took place in Ebenezer Lutheran Church, Columbia, S.C., the ceremony performed by the Rev. P.D. Brown, D.D., pastor of Ebenezer and president of the South Carolina Lutheran Synod.

May 27, 1934, he was ordained into the ministry of the Gospel of the Synod of South Carolina at Mt. Horeb Church, Chapin, S.C.

On June 1st, he entered upon the duties as pastor of the Lexington Lutheran Parish, consisting of the Congregations of Nazareth, Pisgah, Providence, and St. John's. He served this parish until September 29, 1941, on which date he entered the U.S. Army as a chaplain.

For more than four years he served as chaplain of the 63rd Infantry, Sixth Infantry Division. He saw combat service in New Guinea and Luzon, Philippines. He was awarded the Bronze Star Medal for "Meritorious Achievement" during combat in the early days of the Luzon Campaign in 1945. Besides this he wore the American Defense Ribbon with one bronze arrowhead and two campaign stars, the Victory Medal, the Philippine Liberation Ribbon with one bronze star, and was perhaps eligible for others.

After V-J Day he served for three weeks with occupational forces in Korea, returning to the U.S. Dec. 3, 1945. He received his separation papers at Camp Gordon, Ga., Dec. 13, 1945, though not officially discharged until April 8, 1946. In all, he served his country more than four- and one-half years. Twenty-nine months of that service was overseas.

Three wartime poems of his have received some publicity and were well received by the public – "The Christian Soldier's Hymn," "The Chaplain's Duty," and "In Memoriam."

February 15, 1946, he entered upon the duties as pastor of the Bethlehem Lutheran Parish, Irmo, S.C. This parish consisted of the congregations of Bethlehem and St. John's. As pastor and chairman of the building committee, he completed the building of a beautiful new church edifice at Bethlehem, two miles east of Ballentine on National Highway 76.

Legare and Louise had an adopted daughter, Mary Louise. She attended Irmo High School and studied music and voice in Columbia, S. C.

Legare grew up a member of Cedar Grove Lutheran Church, was confirmed in the "old church" by Rev. F.K. Roof. He taught in the Sunday and Daily Vacation Bible Schools while attending college and seminary.

SHERMAN'S RAID DOWN HOLLOW CREEK

Excerpt from J. Ansel Caughman, *History of Religious Life of Cedar Grove Community* (Lexington, SC: Bruner Press, 1952).

William Tecumseh Sherman and his army made a raid through South Carolina in February 1865. They left Savannah, Georgia, about the first of February and travelled north toward Columbia, destroying everything in their path. All the able-bodied men were in the Confederate Army. No one was left to protect the women and children except the aged men and a few dependable slaves.

Most of you have read of the burning and destruction of Columbia about the 17th of February 1865, by Sherman's outlawed army, but very few living people know anything about what happened in the Big Hollow Creek section of Lexington County.

This destructive force travelled in squads covering a wide strip of territory. One group came down one side of this valley and another group came down the other side, laying waste to everything in their path. The inhabitants in this valley heard of the approaching army a few hours in advance. Every person able to travel began to assemble their most valuable possessions together in bundles and hurried to the woods, concealing them from the enemy.

These rebellious soldiers had no mercy on anyone. They would go into the kitchens and smoke houses and bring out barrels of molasses, sauerkraut, flour, and other provisions and pour it all out together in the yards, and then throw shovels of dirt onto it to ruin it. They would carry with them everything that they could in the line of provisions, even great herds of cattle, sheep, and horses. The herds of sheep and cattle were so great they couldn't keep them together. Some would drop out by the wayside and later would be taken up by our people as refugee cattle.

My great-grandmother, Emily Lybrand, was born 1811 and died in 1899. She lived with the Caughmans the last ten years of her life. Often, she would tell me about those tragic days of the Civil War. She said that when Sherman's forces raided their place, there was no one at the house but herself and a neighbor, Dempsey Caughman. She related that a bunch of men rode up to the front gate, all on horseback. One demanded the shot gun. She gave it to them. One took it and broke it to pieces over the gate post. Then they told her to bring them all the gold and silver money. They threatened to burn the house down if she didn't bring it to them. She was slow about moving so they began building a fire under the house. The neighbor ran in the house shouting, "Lord, God Almighty, Emmy, give it to 'em.'" She gave them the two sacks of money. They left immediately without further destruction, except for taking part of the livestock.

By this time, several groups of soldiers had gotten together, moving toward the Saluda River. They stopped next at the plantation of my great-grandfather, Daniel Drafts, who at that time possessed quite a bit of property. He ran about twenty plows. He and his slaves had been able to hide most of the horses in a creek swamp. However, a search began immediately. They went to the big barn, bridled two nice horses, hitched them to the carriage, drove it up to the smoke house and loaded it with meat, getting everything else they wanted that could be found. They set out, crossing Big Hollow Creek, going north on the old Charleston Road toward Holley's Ferry. In traveling up a rough hill the carriage broke down. They loaded the meat on a wagon, rolled the carriage out of the road, bade farewell to the Hollow Creek section.

Practically every settlement from the source of Hollow Creek, near where Leesville now is to Saluda River was molested. Food and livestock were stolen or destroyed, money stolen, clothes and bedding carried away and, in some cases, homes destroyed. . .

When we look back and see what our ancestors had to endure and overcome in establishing homes in a new land, then later passing through the terrible Civil War, losing a large portion of young boys, losing nearly all their earthly possessions, nothing left but the wounded and aged men, widows and orphans to overcome these ravages and repopulate this section and, too, the country was so poor it couldn't provide any kind of pension for the helpless. These things should cause our present generation to begin to take stock and think.

Realizing what our ancestors went through, endured, and overcame, proves to us that they were superior to us. They had no doles or pensions from the government, for the government was too weak for anything like that. The boys and girls of eighty-five years ago made good on their own. Gentlemen, we of the present day, will have to do better than we are doing to compare with our forefathers.

THE JOHN LANGFORD LETTER

Written near Lorena, Lexington County, South Carolina, May 5, 1874, The John Langford Letter was transcribed from the Lyman C. Draper Manuscripts Collection of the State Historical Society of Wisconsin. The John Langford Letter is found in Volume 6VV of the Draper Collection.

Mr. L.C. Draper

Dear Sir:

As far as my memory goes, Lord Rawdon and Col. Cruger, both belonging to the same army, camped at Juniper [Creek] but in the morning separated. Rawdon kept up the direct road to Ninety-Six, and Cruger took up the Lee's Ferry Road.

Col. John Hampton who commanded the Americans, had spies out and engaged him at Weavers' Old Field, to the Big Hollow Creek, crossed, and eluded the fight in what is called Vansants' Old Field. They killed several. I recollect of seeing places shown me by an old lady who said that she and a Miss Weaver went and buried them at three places. There was another place in the Vansant Old Field under a large elm tree, where they [the British] deposited their sick and wounded during their stay there. Several of the wounded died and were buried under the elm tree. The next morning, they took out two men [Thomas and Sylvester Strokes] and took them to a post oak, and while hanging [them], the British took fright and ran off and left them hanging. In about three months after, my father [sic. Actually, it was Mr. Vansant] cut them down and buried their bones.

I have made inquiry of an old gentleman of the name Vansant, who has given me a description of the fight at the Weavers' Old Field between the Americans and British. He says the British were commanded by Lieutenant Colonel Cruger [error, L.C.D.] and as well as my memory serves me, I have heard my stepfather Williams Calk say that the British were six hundred strong, and wounded is uncertain. Mr. Vansant says he has seen four British graves that the occupants were said to have been killed in the fight, and four Americans graves, and the two that he says were left hanging so long on the post oak.

My great uncle Jacob Presnell was in the fight, posted by a tree firing at the British, saying "Dam'em, let 'em come on!" Hampton, seeing he was outnumbered, called a retreat, saying "Boys, follow me!" Presnell, not hearing the order, stood his ground till the enemy was close to him; then looking back for his commander and men and discovering they were gone, he jumped on his unbridled pony, but the animal would not move a step; when he jumped off, seizing one hand in the [text missing].

I remember hearing my father say that he remembered hearing the firing of the guns when Butler and his men were massacred. He and grandmother and uncle were going from a Mr. Gibson's in Lexington County to their home over the line in Newberry, their places of residence being about two miles apart and they are then some ten or twelve [sic] from the bloody scene that enacted. [This was on 7 November 1781, Gandee].

My grandmother Calk [Nancy Presnell Langford, G.S.L.] was married to Grandfather John Langford before the Revolutionary War. Uncle Asa Langford was born in Virginia on the Elizabeth River, and my father was born in the State of Georgia, at or near a place then called Campbelltown, on the Savannah, twelve miles above Augusta, and my grandfather remained at the place [until his] death, caused by a six month's service in the defense of his country at the city of Savannah. After his term of service had expired, he returned to his wife and children, where he soon afterwards died, leaving a widow and two children, Asa, the elder and my father James Langford.

So, I have been told by my grandmother. Grandfather was wounded at what was called the Battle of the Regulation [1771] in Virginia [really in North Carolina – Draper]. He was on the side of Liberty and his life was saved by getting water in the road where it was dry and dusty the day before – the little pool had risen during the night without rain. Shortly after this, grandfather moved to Georgia. After his death, grandmother's father, Daniel Presnell came and took her and the children back to Virginia. Shortly afterward, great grandfather Presnell immigrated to South Carolina and settled on Buffalo Creek in Newberry County about half a mile from great-grandfather Langford, bringing his family, grandmother, and children, which was all done in the time of Revolution. At the breaking out of the war, father was about six years of age, and Uncle Asa between eight and nine.

You asked me to give you an account of other encounters that took place in the surrounding country. David Humes, Benjamin Sullivan, and Luther Holmes came on a parcel of Tories on the war path from Orangeburg to Ninety-Six, at Poplar Springs, taking breakfast and their horses hobbled at grass. Hearing the Whigs coming, the Tories jumped on their horses without stopping to cut or loosen the hobbies. Sullivan soon overtook one whose name proved to be [John] Snellgrove and captured him, while Humes captured one Kennmore [sic], who were jerked off their horses and carried to Senterfeits' Spring and hanged Kennamore with a grape vine and left Snellgrove on his horse with his feet tied under the horse's belly. Hopping Jack [Snellgrove] said the grapevine brook [sic], and down came Kennamore who ran off with one of the Whigs after him and shot and killed him about a quarter of a mile from the place of the hanging. Hopping Jack said, "Old Black's Head [Snellgroves's horse] was for Inman's Island, and he stuck spurs and kept them a digging until he landed safely in the Island. I have heard the old man say, "Poot, begod, I was safe then."

Poplar Springs and Senterfeits' Spring are now owned by Mr. John Price. The two springs are but half a mile apart, one on the south side of the Holly Ferry Road, and the other on the North, lying east and west of the other.

I will now give you an anecdote or daring deed of James Calk, already mentioned, and what brought him and his brother William Calk from the lower country to the upper.

If I mistake not, the affair took place in the Country of St. Matthew's [St. Matthew's Parish, now Calhoun County]. The command that [the Calks] belonged to was attacked by a company of British. James and William and their cousin Dixy Ward were taken prisoners and were being conveyed to the British Post of Moncks Corner. James Calk and the pony he was riding made such an unmilitary appearance that he was not disarmed, and the British captain, who rode up by the side of James Calk and began making fun of him by asking what such a tallow-faced fellow as he was could do – he could not understand what sort of people the Americans were to put children and colts into the field expecting them to do proper service. Nettled by this insolence, young Calk instantly drew his sword and gave the Briton a blow just above the ear, laying him to the road weltering in his gore, while he, putting his spurs to his pony, dashed through the guard and make his escape by lying down on his pony and galloping off [under] the old field pine limbs, which hung so low to the ground that the British could not pursue him, and not thinking to shoot until he was fairly beyond their reach, he make his escape unhurt. His brother and the rest of the prisoners made their escape that night and if I mistake not, the Captain [was] carried to Monck's Corner, and in the time, recovered.

After the escape of the Calks and their friends, they got together and came up the country and joined Captain Walters' Company of mounted rifles, and that caused the Calks to be in on the fight at the Weaver's Old Field between Colonel Hampton and Lord Rawdon's forces.

And James Calk did another daring deed at Eutaw Springs. He went with Captain Walters from the up-country to serve with his countrymen in that memorable struggle, and when the fight brought on, he was eager for the contest, and misunderstanding some order of his commander to charge, he put spurs to his horse with drawn saber, shouting at the top of his voice, "Ye-hoo! By God, let's charge 'em boys!" Dashing through the British lines alone and cutting a British Captain's cap off just above his head, and wheeling his horse, came back through the British lines and regained his command unhurt, though many a shot was fired at him. I have heard this stated for fact by his brother, William Calk, and by Stephen Cumbo of Colonel Samuel Hammond's Command. After the war, James Calk was a great hater of Tories, and had many sore combats with them, and sometimes being overpowered would get [the] worse of it. He was unconquerable as long as he lived. I was at the old man's funeral. The discourse was preached by a Methodist circuit rider by the name of Weathers, as well as my memory serves me. Excuse my long delay and bad spelling and unconnected accounts of these several encounters, for when I received your November letter... [reason not given]

THE LANGFORD NAME

The name "Langford" is an old and well established one. But those bearing the name comprise only a relatively small fraction of the people of this country or England from where American Langfords emigrated. Some of the early freemen of England bore the name. The fact that several parishes in England bear the name indicates men of prominence. One Roger D. Langford was High Sheriff of Cornwall in the year 1225. He took his name from the estate of Langford, in the parish of Marham Church.

In the English countryside of Wiltshire, northwest of the city of Salisbury and not too distant from Stonehenge there is a township and three villages: Little Langford, Steeple Langford and Hanging Langford, that bear the Langford name. Hanging Langford is of interest. Once it so intrigued an American wife with the name that she jumped out of her car, ran across the street, inquiring of those she met – "Where did they hang them? – only to find the village was so named because it was located on the ledge of a high precipice. In southern England alone, ten towns in the eight counties of Bedford, Devon, Essex, Huntingdon, Leicester, Oxford, Somerset, and Wiltshire have the word Langford in association with their name. In London there is a long-established silver gallery with the name. I visited there and bought some silver. The Gallery's brochure, found in the rooms of many hotels, words its invitation – "In the city of London visit Langford's Silver Galleria and 200-year-old Galleries and Treasure Vaults – the Oldest and Largest Silver Showrooms in the World."

Langfords were early emigrants in North America. In 1632, there was

Richard Langford in the Plymouth Colony. Among the early settlers of Virginia were Edward Langford in 1638, Walter Langford in 1643, John Langford in 1651 and Meredith Langford (Henrico County) in 1652. There was a John Langford who settled at Salem, Massachusetts in 1660. Sometime before 1670 there was a Thomas Langford, who made his home in Newport, Rhode Island. The descendants of these and other of more recent establishment have removed to all parts of this nation. They have taken part in its growth and development. Many of them were men and women of affairs. The name is also found in the Canadian Provinces and Central America.

JAMES LANGFORD

The Langfords (English) had adjacent land with the Presnells (French Huguenots), and Nancy Presnell married John Langford. Nancy's father was Jacob, and she had a brother, Jacob. Her husband was killed in a Revolutionary battle and probably buried near Graniteville, South Carolina.

The Langford family by this time had moved down into the Lexington area. Nancy married again to a Calk. She had two children by John Langford: James and Asa. I am descended from that James Langford. My father was the sixth James Langford.

There were several Patriots in the Lexington area. John Langford (Nancy's father-in-law) carried wood and forage to Charleston for the patriots fighting there. Nancy's brother, Jacob, served in the Revolutionary War under Captain Philemon Waters. Nancy's uncle Jacob also served.

At one time the original John Langford took the family back to Virginia, but they returned when so many of them were awarded large tracts of land by the federal government for service in the war. I have copies of these documents.

Hannah Presnell Spencer was born in Edgefield and was the second cousin of Nancy Presnell Langford. Her father was Shepherd Spenser. Hannah's daughter married Dr. Robert Washington who was a popular doctor in Edgefield for many years before moving west.

Genealogical material I found at my trip to Manakin indicated that the Presnell family and the Maupin family were intermarried. The two families were together at Manakin at some time. However, the information about a

Mary Julia Maupin marrying a Presnell was proved to be incorrect.

MANAKIN, VIRGINIA
This information taken from a brochure from the Huguenots Society of Manakin.

Among the earliest European settlers in the [Virginia] Piedmont were several hundred French Huguenots – Protestant religious refugees who had immigrated via London between 1700-1701 on the promise of land from the Crown. They had expected to be settled near existing settlements of Jamestown or lower Norfolk County. Officials gave them land 20 miles above the falls of the James River at areas previously occupied by Native American people. One French settlement in Powhatan County became known as Manakin (after the native tribe).

The colony of Manakin was created by a grant of 10,000 acres of land in Virginia from the English King William III in 1695 to Olivier, Marquis de la Muce, a Huguenot nobleman who ten years earlier had been imprisoned and exiled to England.

Four ships left Southampton for Virginia in the summer of 1699 with a total of more than 500 people. The names of the ships are known – *Pierre and Anthony, Galley of London, Nasseau,* and *Mary and Anne.* Four Huguenot ministers traveled with the expedition; Reverends James Fontaine, Benjamin Joux, Louis Latane and Claude Phillip De Richebourg. The names of surgeons were also known; Dr. Chastine and Paul Micou.

Virginia welcomed the refugees and ex-aristocrats with their education and wealth, brought with them on their immigration from France. The colony exempted the French Huguenots from taxation for a period of seven years. On arriving in Virginia they settled and built homes and plantations out of the wilderness. They also built a church, a school, a hospital, and a black smithy.

The first group of Huguenots encountered great hardships as many were urban people unprepared for the frontier. Their leaders petitioned the government for more assistance as another ship of refugees landed at the Virginia colony. Gradually they adapted and moved out of the villages onto their farms in the area. By 1750 the village was defunct and over the decades the French and their descendants intermarried with English settlers. Many moved west or south to Kentucky and other areas. George Washington was a descendant of Huguenots.

Jacob Presnell, one of the Huguenot Manakin settlers, owned land next to the English Langford family and the two families intermarried. They would several years later move down to South Carolina. This Jacob is my Huguenot ancestor.

MY FRENCH HUGUENOT ANCESTRY

I am very proud of my Huguenot heritage. I believe so deeply that I can interpret the Gospel for myself. I believe salvation comes from faith alone. I have a personal relationship with God. I can speak to Him and not have to go through any other person. This my ancestors believed and why they left everything and came to America.

The Huguenots in France (Reformed Church) grew to about two million people – or about a tenth of all the Christians in the country by 1560. The faith attracted city-dwellers and some of the nobility, who were in general better educated, as well as those in rural regions. It was particularly prevalent in the southern and western parts of France.

In August of 1572, 8,000 to 10,000 Huguenots -- men, women and children -- were killed in the St. Bartholomew's Day Massacre. It was said that the command for the massacre came from the Queen Mother, Catherine de' Medici, of France. This convinced many Huguenots that they had to leave France.

In 1594 Henry of Navarre became king of France – he renounced his Protestant faith and became a Roman Catholic. It is reported that he said, "Paris is worth a mass." However, he issued the Edict of Nantes in 1598 which guaranteed the Huguenots certain religious and civil rights. His descendant, Louis XIV, revoked the Edict of Nantes in 1685, causing many Huguenots to flee.

My French Huguenot ancestor was James Jacob Presnell. He was born in Provence, France, and immigrated to England about 1681 or 1685. He immigrated to Maryland, then to Virginia, and then down to South Carolina.

The first Presnell in America may have been George Prestness (many spellings of the name) at Middlesex County, Virginia, who appears in the records there in the 1680s. James's son, Jacob Presnell, was listed in the Parish Register of Christ Church, Middlesex County, Virginia, as being baptized on March 9, 1708. Son Jacob was baptized on March 14, 1714. James Presnell and Anne Daniel married May 14, 1732. Jacob Presnell died March 4 and was buried March 6, 1716. He married Mary – probably not Mary Maupin as listed at Manakin, but Mary Hedgecock, daughter of Thomas and Margery Hedgecock.

Lois in wedding gown – December 23, 1933.

Grandfather Sansbury.

Grandmother Sansbury.

Lois as a young girl.

3 generations – Lois, Martha Mottie.

Lois and Red at Mottie's debut.

Cousins Peggy Wade Platt, Harriette Wade McElveen and Kathy Wade.

Fletcher with Aunt Crystal, Uncle Bill, Cousin Tom.

Sansbury house in Timmonsville.

Red at school.

Grandmother Langford.

Red with curly red hair on the left with 2 brothers. – Grandmother didn't cut it until he went to school. The family still calls him "Dolly." His nurse lived on the "place" - she was called Blazer.

Grandfather Langford.

Red at Citadel.

Langford picnic – Martha on left seated.

Red's great Grandfather – Confederate soldier killed at Hilton Head.

Cousins Ted, Jane, Sally Fe.

Fletcher with Aunt Sara and Uncle Sleepy.

MILD-MANNERED DR. DERRICK HAD A SECRET LIFE

Before you read our travels (all seven continents) you must realize that my husband, Dr. Fletcher Derrick, was a covert courier for the American Army for some forrty years, carrying the highest security secrets sometimes in dangerous areas. I knew nothing of this. I just thought he was giving medical lectures, which he had been invited to do, but I took advantage of being in certain parts of the world to enjoy neighboring places.

Fletcher was offered this position and association while he was an intern at the hospital in Fort Benning, Georgia. A Colonel told him they had been watching him since high school. He was told that he possessed all the qualities that they needed for someone to do this challenge. He accepted this work with assurance that he wouldn't tell anyone, even his wife. I never knew anything until he wrote his autobiography. I knew that he enjoyed watching spy movies and was very good at keeping secrets.

I had already trained myself to ignore certain things. When I realized I was married to a urologist and that was his specialty, I made a commitment to myself and to him to see that I was never placed in a situation that I would become aware of something that I should not know or tell. If the telephone rang and it was a friend and I determined it was a medical problem, I left the room. He did have some patients to call while we were traveling all over the world. One patient called from Paris and said I must speak with him right now. I made short visits to his office and only when necessary. I find it scary now that "someone" knew where we were always. After his book came out, he told me of his last "drop" when we were in Sicily. We had chosen not to tell anyone of our itinerary. We had a phone on which our family could reach us without knowing where we were. However, someone knew where to always find us.

We went to dinner and when we returned to our hotel room there was a brown envelope on the bed. I thought nothing of it. The next day he suggested we go to mainland Italy, to Anzio cemetery. This is the area in which General Mark Clark led American troops in World War II. He knew as a historian I would enjoy that. At the cemetery he decided to go into the little building there. I did not go. An army major recognized him and approached him for his document. I admire what he did and know it brought great satisfaction to him. When asked to do this, he said to his Colonel, "I never thought that I would be of use to my country in any way except as a doctor."

I know he got great pleasure in knowing that in some way he might have saved a life or made a mission possible.

SEARCHING FOR CONTENTMENT
March 20, 2020

"Fight like hell" – We have certainly heard this a lot lately. But what did it mean to me? A lot. The year 2020 was a bad year for so many people. It was certainly one for me.

My beloved husband of sixty-four years, Dr. Fletcher Derrick, died on March 9 after a long illness. I was devastated and exhausted. After his death, I was in the hospital two different times with serious infections. We were all worried whether I would survive. After each time and after rehab, I was quarantined in my apartment for fourteen days. I spent <u>ninety</u> days by my-self (alone during the pandemic). I was now staying in an assisted living in West Ashley to be near my daughter. I knew I would grieve Fletcher, but not without any family or friends. Nobody could come in; I could not go out. I could not walk in the halls or outside the building. I was very sad and lonely – I was in extreme back pain. I had had four back surgeries and needed another. I did not see my husband's grave for months. My best friend of fifty years died during this time, Loraine Hanckel. I needed her so much. We used to talk on the phone several times a day. We reared children together – went on many fun trips. She left a huge void in my life.

So, what do I do? I thought of some readings: "What does not destroy us, gives us courage" (F. Nietzsche), "Praise God in the midst of adversity" (N. Coward), "I will never leave thee or forsake thee" (Hebrews), "It doesn't matter what happens to man, it is what he does with what happens" (Sophocles). "Be strong and of good courage; be not frightened neither dismayed; for the Lord your God is with you whatever you do" (Joshua 1:9).

Then I thought, "fight like hell" and knew I could do it – but how? Politics: the very thing that was in front of me nearly every minute. I grabbed a yellow legal pad – I went from CNN to FOX and drew a US map and became familiar with all the counties. I stayed up until 3:30 on several nights (one night I was up all night!). We went to Arizona for a medical meeting a year ago – we learned how they loved McCain: Trump said he was no hero because "heroes don't get captured." However, on a trip to Vietnam, we saw where McCain's plane landed – on a lake in front of the house of Ho Chi Minh. There was no escape for him. Trump lost Arizona (slightly). Trump made an unkind statement about Georgia's black congressman who had just died. I watched closely his district of Atlanta and northeast Georgia. Trump lost Georgia and made them count votes three times.

Then I was concerned about Biden. Would he be hurt by some things his son had done? Biden's age would also be a concern. Both Trump and Biden had things to overcome. God's leadership was certainly needed. After the election was over, I started writing this book for my children and grandchildren.

My children moved me to Bishop Gadsden where they provided sessions on grief therapy, which really helped. So, I survived – I fought like hell. My heart will never be the same – "Grief is the price we pay for love" (Queen Elizabeth).

What did I learn? That with God I can do anything! But having so much thrown at me at one time, I was overwhelmed and needed friends. I read a book about grief, and it said, "A widow shouldn't be left alone." That is very true. The days I spent by myself started a week after Fletcher died. COVID was just beginning – nobody could come to see me. My daughter and son made window visits. How I wanted a touch or a hug. I thank God I survived, and my life for now on will be to help others. My cup does run over, and I need to share some of my love and dependence on God. That is the purpose of this book.

Dietrich Bonhoeffer said, "One is less alone when one is alone." I read Psalm 74 often. To me, it means that God sometimes seems slow to us, but it is good timing from God's perspective. It's easy to become impatient for God to act, but I should never give up waiting on Him. When God is silent, I am deep in anguish. I should review the great acts of God through biblical history and then review what He has done for me. This will restore the perspective that God is at work not only in history, but in my life now. Oh – the joy of God's presence.

LIVING IN EUROPE

We had a lovely apartment on the army post at Landstuhl hospital. The western part of the autobahn was right by us. I learned to drive all over Europe. I would invite several friends, and we would spend the day going to lunch in the Officer's Club at Frankfurt, and then we would have a fun time in the antique shops. I bought some beautiful pieces of furniture for about $10.00!

The Derricks were very fortunate to have a wonderful German lady named Irma to act as a nanny for Mottie, who was two years old. She and Irma loved each other and got along beautifully – I was so fortunate. Irma did everything around the house. She spoke no English and I spoke a little German. Fletcher questioned how we got along. Irma said, "We speak our own language." She kept begging to let Mottie spend the weekend with her family. We were reluctant because the German milk was not pasteurized. We finally relented and Mottie loved it. The birth of Mottie when we lived in Baumholder was such a happy event. She was so wanted and so perfect. My family called me Mot and Fletcher called her Mottie.

We made some trips to Berchtesgaden which was where Hitler and his top Generals had homes. The American Army had turned it into a recreational area with wonderful hotels and restaurants. We took the children back there years later. It was so beautiful, and we all gathered the Edelweiss.

To the west there was no autobahn. When we went to Paris or the Netherlands there was only a two-lane road. To go to these places, we always had to go through Belgium and Bastogne. "The Battle of the Bulge" was one place my father wanted to see when my parents visited. We always went to Luxembourg where Patton's grave is located at the head of the troops. My father also wanted to see Dunkirk. We waited in the car while he just walked around the beach thinking of many who died there.

One favorite thing about visiting in this area was seeing so much of Napoleon – Waterloo was always fascinating – and I still can't believe he is entombed in red Russian marble.

THE BERLIN WALL – BEFORE – DURING – AFTER
This first appeared in the Mercury.

Fletcher and I were delighted when he received his army assignment for three years in Germany in 1959. These years were to change our lives completely and instill in us an appreciation for travel. We particularly enjoyed visiting Berlin and were fortunate enough to see it before, during, and after the wall. Our first visit to Berlin was in 1960. Fletcher was then stationed at Baumholder (the largest concentration of troops outside of the United States) as the surgeon for the Eighth Infantry Division Artillery and he was sent to Berlin on an intelligence mission. At that time there was no traveling on the autobahn between West Germany and Berlin. The two ways to reach Berlin were by train or air. We took the train from Frankfurt. The East Germans held up the train for hours because my passport said Martha Langford Derrick and my visa said Martha L. Derrick. It was an overnight trip to Berlin. On the train, Fletcher kept pulling the shade up to see some of East Germany; that terrorized me. While there we visited Phil Walpole from Johns Island and his wife, Margaret Murray, who was a childhood friend of mine. At that time there was free access between West and East Berlin.

We took a tour to the Eastern part and, of course, saw only what they wanted us to see. Many sights were available to us in West Berlin in the American and British sections. We saw Spandau Prison where Speer and Hess were imprisoned; it was later torn down when Hess died in 1987.

Hitler's promise of national greatness ended ultimately with the center of Berlin being 90 percent destroyed. Berlin had suffered greatly from Allied bombing. In one day, 937 bombers of the United States Air Forces accompanied by 600 fighters, bombed the city, and killed 25,000 Berliners.

The rubble from Berlin's destruction during the war was turned into a tremendous hill outside the city. It is still there today – called Devil's Hill – covered with grass and a popular hill to climb, a permanent landscape. It is the highest point in the area.

Before the wall there were many refugees who crossed over to the West bringing nothing with them. I remember accompanying our chaplain with supplies for all those poor families living in barracks with only a hanging sheet dividing them from others. This was the reason the wall went up. The Soviets were losing a great number of intelligentsias from the East, and they could not afford for that to continue. That was a perpetual public relations fiasco for the Soviet camp. A total of 2,689,992 people fled to the West in the period from 1949 – 1961. I found the best shopping in the Kurfürstendamm ("KuDamm," Berlin's main street). People from the East brought their valuables to have extra money and sold them there.

Our second trip to Berlin was when the wall was up. We flew there with our two children who were fascinated by all the security at Checkpoint Charlie. The wall went up in August 1961. It literally was built from sunrise to sunset. Margaret Walpole remembers one man laying brick while another man with a gun watched him and another man with a gun watched that one. The number of deserters (who made it) would end up being around 2,000.

I don't believe people who were not in Germany at that time realized how close we came to war. Khrushchev was in power, and Gary Powers had just been shot down and imprisoned.

On August 13, 1961, tanks from the East German army had taken up position on the Unter Den Linden to block off the Brandenburg Gate. Our armed forces in West Berlin had a silent parade with only drums sounding and people watching, to show that West Berliners and the American army intended to protect their part of the city. Washington, too, wanted to calm the fears and dispatched Vice President Lyndon B. Johnson to Berlin to deliver a message from President Kennedy. West Berlin's freedom and free access to East Berlin for the western powers were guaranteed. At that same time a motorized battalion of 1,500 men was sent across East Germany along the access routes to West Berlin to strengthen the garrison there – a symbolic step, intended to strengthen the psychological power of resistance in West Berlin.

When our troops started marching through East Germany, our army was on the highest alert. Fletcher was called at 2:00 a.m. and told to come – this was no training exercise. His mission was to command the train going to Helmstedt, the town at the border between the East and West autobahn and to bring the wounded back to Landstuhl where he was now stationed. Landstuhl is the U.S. military medical center for Europe and the Middle

East. (This is where our troops were sent who were wounded in Iraq and Afghanistan).

When he left that morning, Fletcher told me to get out of Germany. At the bottom of the Landstuhl hill was the Miesau ammunition depot with missiles aimed at East Germany. I knew that would be the first target from the East. I was totally afraid to make any move. The evacuation route for dependents was a two-lane highway to Paris. We dependents were required to always keep a can of gas and other supplies in case of an emergency. I had a friend in Switzerland, and I decided to go there. Somewhat later Fletcher reminded me Switzerland was a neutral country. They would not have let me inside their borders. And if I got there, and there was a war, I could have to stay there until the war ended.

Sometime ago, the commander of Baumholder decided to have a practice of the emergency evacuation for dependents. When the Germans saw all the Americans leaving with their children and animals, they thought it was the real thing and joined the caravan. It was a nightmare. It was apparent that in case of war, getting out of Baumholder was practically impossible.

In Landstuhl now, I suddenly realized there were no other lights on in the housing area. One helicopter pilot had come down our stairwell and disappeared. I had to use some levity and reality for myself to realize we could not be fighting the Russians with Fletcher and one helicopter pilot.

Due to a bizarre set of circumstances, the rest of the medical support personnel in our area, which included helicopters, ambulances, etc., were not notified until five hours later. A serious investigation ensued.

It was a dreadful time for me – no radio or TV was available. I did not see or hear from Fletcher for almost ten days. The doctors assigned to the hospital came by and offered help while Fletcher was gone. Margaret Walpole was going through a much worse situation in Berlin. Her husband was now the aide to the General there.

The threatened major crisis was defused after several horrible weeks. When the wall was completed, there became a stalemate that was going to persist until the wall came down on November 9, 1989.

On our second trip to Berlin, our family was house guests of Colonel

Edward Hamilton from James Island and his wife, Jane. We knew Ed had a secret mission behind the wall that could not be discussed then. He graduated from West Point and taught Russian there and was the perfect one for the mission. He had to cross the Glienicke Bridge (Gary Powers was exchanged for a Soviet spy there) to Potsdam in East Berlin, where the Americans had a house according to an agreement among the four powers. The Soviets had a comparable mission in the West.

Ed said it was the difference of night and day to pass from West Berlin to East Berlin. It was like someone had pulled a curtain. There were few people out, no flowers, and a few cars spouting black fumes, and blocks of black square houses. A woman at the U.S. mission house prepared sandwiches and coffee for them before they drove for two days through East Germany – sleeping in the car in the woods at night (out of sight).

This mission was to find out whether the East Germans were simply having maneuvers or really gearing up for war. In other words, was the Cold War about to become a hot war? They made lists, photographs, and observed Russian military activities and weapons. The East Germans knew they were there, and once Ed's car was rammed by a truck. He was seriously injured.

This was highly classified work. Sometimes we had more than one mission through East Germany – a great risk – but it was for highly needed surveillance. The Cold War Museum at Warrenton, Virginia, dedicated to United States liaison missions, was established in 1969 by Gary Powers, Jr.

Our third and fourth visits to Berlin were after the wall came down. The reunited city was now ablaze with lights and activity. We met our Orangeburg friend Henry Bair. He had studied there for many years and was a perfect tour guide.

There were hundreds of cranes in the 1990s – Berlin was the largest construction site in the world at that time. All those horrible dark, drab Soviet buildings were torn down.

The Brandenburg Gate is now surrounded by exciting new architecture. Unter den Linden is a promenade around the gate. A boulevard has been created with many businesses and embassies. The city bureaucracy adopted elaborate procedures to control re-building. There are no skyscrapers. There was little attempt to duplicate what had been there. The people wanted a "new city." They wanted it to symbolize future Germany. The new architecture is magnificent.

The city is particularly rich in museums. The French Huguenot Church (*Französischer Dom*) the oldest part of which was built in 1701, was heavily damaged during the war. It was totally rebuilt between 1977 and 1981. The Reichstag was completely restored with a magnificent glass dome, and it has once again become the home of the German Parliament, the Bundestag. There is nothing anywhere like the artifacts in the Pergamum Museum.

The main attraction now is the new Holocaust Memorial. It is in the middle of Berlin, and you enter it on the same level as the street. The architect for the memorial was Daniel Libeskind who also won the competition for the rebuilding of the area of the World Trade Center. The grid pattern, consisting of 2,711 concrete gray-colored times can be walked through from all sides. It leaves visitors to find their own way in and out of the complex. We walked up the stairs of a nearby building to see it from above, and I realized what I (Martha) was seeing – the caskets for Jews that were never used. It was a profound moment for me.

Angela Merkel, of the Christian Democratic Union party, was Chancellor of Germany from 2005 to 2021. She had a complicated background, having lived in East Germany during her childhood. Her father was a Lutheran minister, and she has a doctorate in physical chemistry. She was from a conservative background, and it is remarkable how she had held things together. Merkel lost the last election, and Olaf Scholz, a Social Democrat, was chosen as Chancellor.

Growing together has been difficult for some Berliners. Some still have feelings of the old regime and say, "You should have seen things when the Soviets had it," meaning how much better it was.

The Eastern region, after reunification, was dependent on subsidies funded by Western Germany. Billions in Western German assistance has been received since 1990. Fundamental things were done after reunification that the Soviets never did. There are many roads and railroads being built, for instance.

I took a course in German in 1960 and the first thing I was told was, "Bonn was chosen as the West German capital of divided Germany because it was so insignificant it would never be considered as the true capital of a united Germany." Since the wall came down, the capital of Germany has returned to Berlin. This great city is once again taking its place as a leading city of the world. Having been a participant and observer of sixty-plus years of changes in Berlin makes it very special to me and my family.

TRIER
Karl Marx

Born in Trier, the ancient city was then part of the Kingdom of Prussia's provinces of the lower Rhine. His family was originally non-religious Jewish but had converted to Christianity before his birth.

His wife, Jenny, was also born in Trier. Her family was influential and wealthy and many times when Marx was not making much money, Jenny returned to her family in Trier for help. There was one time when the Marx family was penniless. Jenny pawned her last piece of jewelry, and they were now dependent on a public collection among Marx's Rhineland friends.

Marx and High Gate Cemetery

Fletcher and I had many trips to England, but one time we went for him to study a new surgical procedure. I had a guide to see the English houses. They were so much like Charleston's Nathanial Russell House. Then I wanted to see where Marx was buried. We wandered around High Gate cemetery and found a most impressive huge monument containing some things from his writings. "Religion is the opiate of the masses." We turned to leave the cemetery and saw four men approaching us. I knew they were Eastern Europeans because of the old suits they wore. They were coming toward us in the huge cemetery where we were alone. My guide panicked. I calmed her down and we pressed on. I said "Good day" in German. My guide remarked she never wanted another person who wanted to see High Gate cemetery!

According to Wikipedia.org: "Many intellectuals, labour unions, artists, and political parties worldwide have been influenced by Marx's work, with many modifying or adapting his ideas. Marx is typically cited as one of the principal architects of modern social sciences."

Trier was the northernmost city of the Roman Empire and contains Roman ruins. It was a delight to visit.

Washington Days

When Fletcher told me he had accepted the position as professor and chairman of the Department of Urology at George Washington University, I was elated. I thought it was a good professional move, and I was excited about living in Washington, D.C. Everything turned out to be good for all our family.

We bought a nice home in McLean, Virginia, across the highway from the CIA. (The highway sign read "Turkey Run Experimental Station.") The house was also across from the home of Ethel Kennedy. Our children were invited to several parties over there, and that was such fun for them. Andy Williams brought the Kennedy children to our neighborhood one Halloween.

The exciting thing for me was the McLean Baptist Church. So many members were leaders in our nation's government – extremely intelligent people. Fletcher was in a Sunday school class that consisted of mostly CIA staffers. They said they worked for the State Department, but they were gone for months at the time, and we all knew better. The vasectomy was just becoming popular. When they found out Fletcher was a urologist, they kept pestering him for a "group rate"!

Tom, the minister, and his wife became such good friends. They asked us – legally – to rear their child if something happened to them (what an honor!). I was teaching Sunday school and had many informative chats with Tom. He was brilliant – nothing but A's in his academic career – University of Richmond, SE Seminary, PhD, Johns Hopkins ("Near Eastern History"). Our son Carl and I went on one of his Holy Land trips, and I think Carl for the first time found the love of God. I was in an element I only dreamed of all that history around me.

There was a Thurmond South Carolina Club in the D.C. area, and we were invited to many events. U.S. Senator Strom Thurmond and his family lived around the corner from us, and I became Nancy's assistant when the senator was unable to attend a function. It was fun parking that car with the senatorial license plate anywhere in the city. I was given special tickets to the State of the Union addresses, which I always enjoyed.

FROM OUR WASHINGTON DAYS
INTEGRITY UNDER PRESSURE (A WATERGATE HERO)
This appeared in the Mercury.

When we think of Watergate we think of lust for power, clandestine moments, secrets, devious untruths, indictments, prison, and the resignation of a president. But have you ever thought of Watergate producing a positive outcome of extreme integrity under pressure? I would like to tell you a story that didn't make headlines. It is a shining example of good amid all the bad in the Watergate scandal.

It was our pleasure when we lived in the Washington area to have a friendship with Johnnie Mac Walters and his wife, Donna. Walters was born in Darlington County and graduated from Hartsville High School, Furman University and received his L.L.B. degree from Michigan Law School after World War II. He was an officer in the United States Air Force and flew fifty combat missions from Italy. Many honors were given him including the Purple Heart and the Distinguished Flying Cross. In 1949, Walters was appointed to a job in the Chief Counsel's office with the Internal Revenue Service in Washington. After working there five years and with the Legal Department of Texaco Incorporated in New York City for another eight years, Walters moved to Greenville, South Carolina, and entered private practice. He specialized in federal tax law and was active in the Tax Section of the American Bar Association and the South Carolina Bar.

Then his life took a different turn. He received a phone call on January 2, 1969, informing him that he was one of two people being considered as a possible nominee to head the Tax Division of the Department of Justice. The Attorney General Designate – John Mitchell – wanted an immediate answer. Walters' wife and his law partner (B.F. Geer, Jr.) agreed this was a great opportunity for a tax lawyer since the position of Assistant Attorney General in charge of the Tax Division was one of the greatest positions in the world for a tax lawyer. He told his contact he was available, but would not politic for the job. It was never known exactly who suggested him as a nominee. Through the years he had attended many Republican meetings but was not very active in the political world.

It was suggested that he call Senator Strom Thurmond since the Senator had been instrumental in helping elect President Nixon. Senator Thurmond was told by Walters he would be available if the administration thought he would be helpful but once again, he would not politic for the job. The Deputy Attorney General Designate informed Walters that the job was his, and he was to report to the Department of Justice on January 9, 1969. Senator Thurmond's office announced the nomination while Walters was still in New York, having gone there for the interview with John Mitchell. Shortly after Walters' nomination, Senator Fritz Hollings offered him advice that later proved to be very helpful in dealing with Capitol Hill.

For three years the Tax Division was quite enjoyable. He dealt with outstanding tax lawyers and with significant tax issues. The Solicitor General had him argue two cases before the Supreme Court, which he won.

When the position of Commissioner of Internal Revenue became available in 1971, Attorney General John Mitchell asked Walters if he would be willing to serve as Commissioner and he agreed. Once again, Walters was a willing public servant. The Senate confirmed the nomination and he served from 1971 to 1973 at the helm of the IRS. As Commissioner of IRS, he administered tax laws world-wide with about 110,000 employees.

Walters immediately took appropriate action to speed up the auditing of returns. He was told that on individual returns, the IRS was several years behind and that some large corporation cases were not closed for twelve years. Walters instructed his Assistant Commissioner (Compliance) to develop a plan to audit the returns, including those of large corporations, promptly. Large corporations were unhappy with this because they were required to pay only 6 percent interest on IRS liabilities whereas interest rates at the time were running in the high teens. So, they were making money on their liabilities owned the IRS. One large corporation paid the government about fifty million dollars as the IRS closed its audit. Walters tried to observe the statutory responsibility to collect revenue as fairly as he could and to treat taxpayers alike regardless of who they were. His aim was to treat everybody as gently as possible while collecting the revenue due. But Commissioner Walters did not make many friends!

Walters is best known for what he did not do. There was a White House spy in his office who was concerned about payments from the Howard Hughes International Corporation to the chairman of the Democratic Party, Larry O'Brien. The IRS had audited Mr. O'Brien's returns and found that he had reported all amounts received, and the IRS had refunded to him a small overpayment. The White House representative still expressed concern and wanted even more information. Again, Walters advised the White House that under IRS policy, nothing more could be done.

When the White House asked yet again for additional information, the spy was confronted, and Walters, along with George P. Schultz, the Secretary of the Treasury, reviewed the case by telephone with John Ehrlichman, who was the White House Counsel and Assistant to the President for Domestic Affairs, for President Richard Nixon. Ehrlichman told Walters that he was tired of his "foot-dragging tactics." This led Walters to emphatically inform Secretary Schultz that he could have his job any time he wanted it.

Then came the "Enemies List." Walters received a call from John Dean, Counsel to the President, inviting Walters to come to his office. After Walters and Dean had a friendly visit, Dean handed him an envelope containing a list of about 20 Democrats that the White House wanted "investigated and thrown in jail."

Walters was absolutely appalled and stunned. The 1972 election would be coming up in a very few months. At this time, Walters did not know what Watergate was, but Dean did. Then Walters said he made a big mistake. He walked out with the list. The list should have been left with Dean and refused immediately. Walters informed Secretary Schultz that, in his opinion, the IRS should do absolutely nothing with the list. It would ruin the integrity of the tax system. Walters told the Secretary that he was going to lock the list in the Commissioner's safe and do nothing further. Walters then personally sealed the list so it would be obvious if ever opened and locked it in his safe without telling his personal secretary or his deputy. No one at the IRS knew he had the list.

Later, John Ehrlichman testified before a Congressional committee that the White House had given Walters the list. Walters then voluntarily delivered it to Larry Woodworth who headed the staff of the Joint Committee on Taxation. Woodworth now could say, with absolute certainly, that the IRS never began any investigation of any name on that list. Walters pointed out that he had sealed it personally and that it had never been opened. He testified and admitted that John Dean had called him twice and asked what progress had been made. Walters advised him both times that no action had been taken.

Walters believes this is the most important thing he did as Commissioner because if he had acted on the request, respect for our tax system would have been ruined. "I did not want to diminish the role of Commissioner because I believe that job is very important to the nation. I am convinced that our tax system is the very basis of our republican form of government, and it is essential to our whole governmental system. It should be operated properly, and I am convinced that if our tax system fails, we will find ourselves amid civil disorder. Just think what might happen if the government could not make Social Security payments, pay judges, pay Congress, and could not meet its obligations generally. Although imperfect, I know no other part of government as basic as our tax system."

Johnnie Walters wanted the Secretary of the Treasury and others above him to have complete confidence in him and trustworthiness of his independence. He would not buckle under to political pressure. He refused to be a tool of the White House. He had not accepted his position to obtain power. In 1973, he resigned and returned to private practice.

During this interview, I asked Walters some questions and here are his answers:

Q: How much contact did you have with the President and the White House?

A: "Very little." He and Donna did attend some functions at the White House and met the Nixons personally. He was in the Oval Office several times. Never did he have any conversations with the President about his position or duties. On one of the Nixon Tapes, Nixon is heard saying, "Walters is refusing to cooperate – we should kick him out and get another man in there."

Q: Why do you think that Watergate happened?

A: "Power – pure lust for power." These people let blind loyalty rule their decisions. Placing loyalty above judgement can be a hazardous thing.

Q: Did you fear for your job?

A: "No. I was there to serve my country." He would not let his position be compromised. Public servants have high responsibilities to behave and do what is right. He would do the same again today. Public service is a wonderful opportunity. He smiled but was firm in his decision. He volunteered to appear before a grand jury and appeared before several congressional committees. He was pleased to tell exactly what happened. The Watergate grand jury voted not to indict him and there was no penalizing action.

Q: Why did you not use the "Enemies List?"

A: "My parents taught me to do the right thing always regardless of the circumstances." His parents were good and decent people. He put the list in his safe, locked it, and neither he nor anyone else at the IRS ever looked at it.

This is truly an example of integrity under pressure. In troubling times, Johnnie Mac Walters rose to the zenith of courage and honor.

Addendum

The Derricks and the Walters attended the same church in McLean, Virginia. One day the minister preached (shaking his finger at the congregation), "not everyone around Jesus Christ was good – there were harlots and tax collectors and other bad people." Following the sermon, as he was leaving the church and shaking hands with the minister, Walters jokingly asked for the minister's social security number. The minister and all concerned have had many laughs over that incident.

Nancy Thurmond

As I wrote in my personal history, I was named for Senator Thurmond's sister, Martha Thurmond Bishop. Our families remained close through the years. "Big Martha" had four sons. She always wanted a little girl, so she let me play that part in her life.

Nancy and the Senator were our neighbors in McLean, Virginia, just up the parkway from the city. We happened to have children the same age – our Carl and their Nancy Moore were about four years old when we moved to McLean. Our families took our children to special events. Carl and Nancy Moore especially enjoyed a little carnival near our house. We went to the big circus in the city. We were enjoying ourselves when we missed the Senator – we found him riding an elephant!

Nancy and I became very close. She was lonely and needed a companion to go places when the Senator was occupied with political occasions. She would come for me in that car with the Senatorial license plate. As we rode off, Fletcher wondered if he would ever see us again!

Nancy told people I was her "best friend in Washington." She loved for me to go shopping with her, one of my favorite things. We attended a lovely tea for the Vice-President's wife, and club meetings where Nancy was President and Jackie Kennedy's mother (a lovely lady) was Vice President.

I learned a great deal from her and am so grateful for time spent with her. After I left Washington her life became so sad with the death of her daughter, Nancy Moore. I still see her from time to time.

GENE POTEAT

Oh, what a special person! He and his wife Martha were our neighbors in McLean, and we attended the same church. We quickly became good friends because we had so much in common.

S. Eugene Poteat was reared in Charleston, served in World War II, and then graduated from The Citadel with a B.S. degree in electrical engineering. He earned a Master's degree in statecraft and national security affairs with a specialization in intelligence studies from the Institute of World Politics in Washington, D.C., and was awarded an honorary LL. D for his service to intelligence education and the intelligence profession.

Gene worked at Bell Telephone Laboratories and at Cape Canaveral, where he designed missile guidance systems. During the Cold War, he was recruited by the Central Intelligence Agency, with which he worked on the U-2 spy aircraft and designed a cloaking system for the Lockheed Martin SR-71 aircraft. In the Directorate of Science and Technology, he provided scientific expertise on space and naval reconnaissance systems. He also served at the National Reconnaissance Office.

During the Cuban missile crisis, the CIA quickly pulled Gene from Eastern Europe to Miami. He knew more about Russian missiles than anybody else. He was in touch with President John F. Kennedy and advised him along the way to a peaceful resolution.

He managed the CIA's worldwide network of intelligence monitoring sites and received numerous CIA awards for excellence in service to his country.

When we came to know Gene, we were told he was with the State Department. He was gone from McLean for months at a time. Everybody knew he was CIA and involved with intelligence about Russia and Eastern Europe.

Fletcher and I kept in touch with him. One time we were coming home from Nigeria and contacted Gene who met us in London. He was the best guide we had ever had. He knew all the wonderful restaurants and we attended a fabulous concert in Prince Albert Hall with him. He was a gifted musician.

When we moved back to Charleston, Gene came back into our lives. He had family here and he stayed close to The Citadel. My Sunday School class was always thrilled when he came and talked about spies in the Bible, especially women spies.

We had him in our home often and invited guests who would enjoy Gene and who he would enjoy.

Gene died May 22, 2020. We lost a good friend and a great American.

Will Cathcart and other writers for the Charleston *Mercury*, had a meeting with Gene in 2008, when the newspaper was preparing to cover the Russian invasion of the Republic of Georgia. Cathcart recalled, "Gene Poteat had an intelligence that was contagious. Without him, the evils and injustices of this world seem overwhelming. Gene never gave away any secrets; back then. There were few to give on Putin's plans for Georgia, but Gene had a way of grinning – beaming – that led us to believe we were on the right track."

Following Gene's death, Cathcart wrote, "I feel as though I've lost a guardian angel. Gene will be dearly missed. But a great deal of good will be done in his memory. A world without Gene Poteat is a less secure, less elegant, and less informed world. And yet I suppose that Gene would say that this is precisely why it is up to us now to address those evils and injustices head-on and without hesitation."

First visit to Charleston with Father and Grandmother.

At Mottie's debut.

First grade trip to Rowesville on the train. I am on the left in dark dress.

25th wedding anniversary –
Versailles, Paris.

Martha in Coker May Court.

Wedding.

Martha and Fletcher dating in
Charleston.

2 Doctors – Carl's Medical School Graduation.

Fletcher as Clemson cadet.

Martha's home – 895 Broughton Street, Orangeburg.

High School friends: Bert Gue, West Summers, Pat Duncan.

2 Gibbes Street, Charleston. We lived there 20 years.

Fletcher's favorite beach thing with Eliza and Ron.

Our first apartment in Charleston – 25 ½ Gadsden Street.

With residents he had at George Washington University.

Fletcher's roses in church with Pat Dennis, Myrtle Ann was arranger.

50th Medical Class Reunion.

Top of Kilimanjaro.

Presenting PH.D. as Clemson Trustee.

Viewing the troops as President of the Charleston Chamber of Commerce.

First rose he painted – Candlelight.

His roses arranged by him in his vase.

Fletcher as a baby with sister, Betty.

Our home in McLean, Virginia.

RETURN TO CHARLESTON

The position at George Washington was very important to Fletcher. His cousin, Butler Derrick, was in the House of Representatives. He sent capitol workers to Fletcher for treatment. He also treated some members of the Supreme Court. He was asked to be a consultant to the Surgeon General, especially working at the Walter Reed Army Medical Center. He helped give the national exam for urology.

But something was wrong. Fletcher came home one day and said, "I told the Dean today I was resigning. He said I could not do that – I had tenure and such an important position. I told him I was doing too much administrative work, and what I wanted to do was the 'big surgery', and I wanted a one-to-one relationship with the patients." That was where his love of medicine was, and where he thought he had the most talent. I was crushed and cried. I had known we were not going to be there forever – but …

We were all excited and elated to be going home after all this moving and traveling to be with friends we had when we were young and enjoy family gatherings – and to worship in the church that meant so much to us.

We rented a house at 2 Gibbes Street – built in 1830-35 by Robert Fenwick Giles. Giles had a prolific garden on that property – especially with fruit. Little did he know that in the next century, a doctor living on the property had a rose garden. It had 3 stories – 7,500 square feet. The night we moved in Johnny Hanckel told Carl the house was haunted. Carl would not sleep on the third floor unless Mottie was with him. It was located a block from the Battery. We had plans to build on a lot there. Suddenly, the owner wanted to sell 2 Gibbes. He said he had a list of people who wanted to buy it, and he put us second on the list. There was no negotiating the price. We had learned to really love the house and bought it when the first people declined.

Mottie enrolled in Ashley Hall and had a wonderful experience there. She particularly loved the sewing course, being a soloist in the Red choir and the excellent English classes. She graduated from Clemson and then studied at the Fashion Institute in New York. She has four children: Eliza, Ron, Derrick, and Owen plus two grandchildren, Louise, and Katherine.

Carl had to wait several years for a space to open at Porter-Gaud. He thought it was the "promised land" – a great group of friends. He excelled in all athletics- was quarterback for the football team and played soccer. He went to Hampden Sydney with his friends, and it was a good choice for him since he played collegiate soccer. He then went, like Fletcher, to the Medical University in Charleston. He is now an Internist in Beaufort. He has three boys: Heyward, Crosson, and Stuart. Someone told Fletcher one time that all those "damn Southerners have two last names."

We lived at 2 Gibbes for 20 years and then moved to a smaller house at 12 Orange Street which was built in 1770. It had six fireplaces and was so charming. We spent 20 years there. Fletcher and I are ardent preservationists. We modernized both houses with new baths and kitchen. We were very active in the Historic Charleston Foundation - letting them show our houses in spring and Preservation Society in fall. That is 40 years of giving back to the community. Fletcher had a lovely rose garden (about 100 bushes) in each place. During the tours he could be found in the garden – loving it when someone asked him about growing roses!

Our children were not pleased when the house was on tour. I'd say, "Don't leave that there" – "Put that away," "Disappear for four hours!" We found a solution – the whole family would go out for a long dinner at a nice restaurant. That seemed to please them.

We were both active in the community. Fletcher was President of the Chamber of Commerce, President of the Charleston County Medical Society, a Clemson University Trustee and member of the Trustee Board at the Charleston Museum and Chairman of Deacons at First Baptist Church. I was President of the Charleston Garden Club, President of County Medical Auxiliary, and a trustee at Coker College.

The Charleston Museum is responsible for two houses – the Manigault House and the Heyward-Washington House. One day I was standing on the piazza of the Manigault house and noticed that the beautiful garden had a chain-link fence on the east side. Something had to be done. We had bought bricks to build a house and did not need them anymore. So, we donated them to the Manigault house for a matching wall on that side. I found a bricklayer who had done some work on the other wall. It was beautiful!

I was very interested in the Heyward house since three of our grandsons had a Heyward mother who was a direct descendant of the builder – Thomas Heyward, Jr. I had a secret friend and used him to repair some of the beautiful furniture there. The museum director was the only one who knew I was doing this, and he was so pleased to point out a crack here, a dent there, a scratch or a piece missing. I didn't do much but got great satisfaction to help.

Yes, we still traveled, but it was so peaceful to come back to the place where you belonged. "No person whatsoever shall disturb, molest, or persecute another for his speculative opinion in religion, or his way to worship." That is so exciting to live in such a city.

So, with all the traveling and moving we did, Charleston is where we ended our lives. Fletcher is buried on a peninsula on the Cooper River, and every time I cross the Ravenel Bridge, I throw him a kiss!

GINKGO

We had a lovely ginkgo at 2 Gibbes. Its golden leaves all fell in one day. The bad thing is that it was a female tree that dropped these terrible-smelling fruits. We always had to apologize when visitors came in the garden at that time. Hurricane Hugo in 1989 damaged some of its limbs and it lost some of its shape. We had a white cat named Frosty who only made an appearance in the tree when there were guests in the garden. She put on quite a show.

A symbol of hope and a testament to longevity, Ginkgo possess a history that rivals no other plant. Fossils show that these tenacious trees have been around for about 250 million years, even outlasting the dinosaurs. A single tree planted now can live for well over a thousand year – good news for even the most neglectful gardener. In the spring, its glossy green leaves make an attracting tree in the landscape, but it's in the fall that the Ginkgo really shines. The lobed leaves radiate a golden glow, and when the wind brushes by, the tree looks as if a million butterflies have alighted on its branches. When the show is over, the leaves will drop within a day or two, leaving behind a pool of gold – making it easy to rake them up in one afternoon. -- *Southern Accents*, September/October 2008, p. 66.

A CONSTITUTION FOR "CAROLINA"

John Locke, the philosopher, was a good friend of Lord Ashley Cooper (the Lord Proprietor who took the most interest in the colony.) He wrote the Fundamental Constitutions for Carolina in 1669 which said to vote or become a citizen all you had to do was worship God. It didn't matter which way you worshipped. So, we had one of the widest measures of religious freedom in early Carolina, more than other colonies. This made in a big difference in my own life – as my ancestors felt free and welcomed to come here.

Of course, the first people to come were the Episcopalians. Then in 1682, the Baptists who had been worshiping in Kittery, Maine, came and established the first southern Baptist Church. Several denominations met in the Meeting House on Meeting Street, on the site of the Circular Congregational Church. The Presbyterians moved from there to First (Scots) Presbyterian in 1731. French Catholics came in the late 18th century when there was a slave rebellion in Saint Domingue, joined by Irish Catholics, and established St. Mary's in Hasell Street. The graveyard of the Quakers is located under the Charleston County garage on King Street. The Methodists preached against slavery and had more converts in Savannah. Sephartic Jews from Spain and Portugal were granted the rights of Englishmen. The "cradle" of Reform Judaism in America is here in Charleston.

A prominent 19th century Jew was Judah P. Benjamin – a Sephartic Jew born in the Caribbean, who spent his early life in Charleston. His parents had a fruit stand on King Street where Kerrison's department store was later built. He attended Yale but was expelled (possibly an anti-Semitic act). He then practiced law in New Orleans – had a brilliant career there – and married into an old French family. He was Secretary of War – and then Secretary of State of the Confederacy. He was not captured with Jefferson Davis but escaped to Florida – then to England where he became a barrister for Queen Victoria. He died in France where he was living with his wife and daughter.

All South Carolina should be proud of this part of our history – an early granting of religious liberty and freedom of conscience.

FLETCHER DERRICK, SILVER HONOR MEDAL WINNER
American Rose Magazine

In ceremonies at the Carolina District Winter Meeting in Wilmington, N.C., on January 31, 2009, the prestigious Silver Honor Medal was presented to Dr. Fletcher Derrick in recognition of his extraordinary contributions to the American Rose Society and the Carolina District. The Silver Honor is the highest award that may be presented in the district that includes North and South Carolina.

Lynn Stevens, District Awards Chair, made the presentation, citing many of Fletcher's contributions to the ARS, district, and local programs. Fletcher has been an ARS member since 1972 and is the recipient of the district's Outstanding Rosarian Award and the Bronze Medal of the Charleston Low-country Rose Society. He has served as president and vice president of the South Carolina Rose Society as well as the Charleston Lowcountry Rose Society. He is an ARS Horticulture Judge, Cyber Rosarian, Master Rosarian, and active participant in district and local rose society activities. He has given numerous presentations on various facets of rose culture at all levels and has served as faculty at District Consulting Rosarian Schools.

Fletcher Derrick and Peggy Heinsohn are the cofounders of the Charleston Lowcountry Rose Society. They were teaching, talking roses, and giving lectures on the Charleston scene before our society was founded! They are our first Consulting Rosarians, and their leadership continues to this day.

Fletcher's teachings and programs have brightened garden center and garden club events and meetings of rose societies locally and throughout the southeast. He has served as teacher, lecturer, promoter, salesman, mentor, and advisor to anyone interested in roses. His sunny disposition and upbeat personality make communication easy. He takes every opportunity to teach others the art of growing beautiful roses.

He is also a talented artist who paints roses; his paintings are on display in galleries in Charleston and adorn the walls of many offices and private homes.

Fletcher's passion for growing and showing beautiful roses has no equal in Charleston. His beautifully maintained garden of 150+ roses is a perfect showcase for the roses he grows in the ground, in pots, on trellises, and high over the walls around it. He delights in opening his garden to visitors to downtown Charleston and to garden clubs and other horticultural groups.

Fletcher Derrick is a complete rosarian. He has demonstrated extraordinary leadership, expertise, and outreach skills through three decades of service to the community and the Carolina District. The Silver Honor Award recognizes this lifetime of service and devotion to roses.

Previous CLRS Silver Honor winners are Peggy Heinsohn, Frances Ballentine, Sandy Lundberg, and Bob Lundberg. Congratulations, Fletcher Derrick! We are so proud of your achievements, and this deserved recognition.

MEDICAL MALPRACTICE – A FAMILY NIGHTMARE

Our nightmare began on Halloween, 1987. It was an early Saturday morning, and my husband was making hospital rounds. I was sleeping late when the doorbell rang. I was handed a public complaint. After pouring my coffee, I started to read. At first, I thought it was a Halloween joke. The more I read, the more I realized it was anything but a Halloween joke.

The malpractice suit in which my husband was charged may have been more traumatic and emotional than others. Because, you see, the plaintiffs were a local doctor and his wife. They were friends whom we had enjoyed and admired.

My husband was not the primary doctor named in the suit. He was a co-defendant. He never saw the plaintiff as a patient. His involvement was because of a prescription for pain medicine which he had called in and not recorded in the plaintiff's chart, and he assisted in the surgery. He made no decision in the diagnosis or the treatment of the patient. For this we were to endure 15 months of stress and 5 days of "hell" during trial.

I say "we" because a malpractice suit affects the entire medical family. This is especially true when you are married in medical school and always referred to that experience as "when we were in medical school." The association with medicine had become a joint venture of two lives.

Malpractice suits didn't happen to people who worked hard for their patients. My husband is too good a doctor. He is a compassionate man who loved the one-on-one relationship with his patients. We, like others, hoped we were immune from such a thing.

But it did happen to us, and it was without a doubt the most traumatic, emotional experience our family had ever faced. We have both lost parents, but that did not compare to this. The death of parent is expected in life. But whoever expects to be sued by a fellow physician and his wife – friends of many years? There is no preparation for this.

Our friends were wonderful to us. They treated the situation as if a death had occurred. They brought food to the house, wrote us notes and sat through the trial with us. When they asked if I wanted them there, I truly did not know what I wanted. But their presence certainly helped.

Several urologists reviewed the case for us. They came to the prompt conclusion that there was no basis for the case. Two of them willingly gave generously of their time and expert knowledge and, at great inconvenience to themselves, agreed to come to court and serve as expert witnesses.

The expert witness for the plaintiff was a urologist who had practiced in Charleston until 1966. He then moved to another state. He retired in Charleston about six years prior to the trial. He asked my husband to sponsor his membership in the County Medical Society when he returned to Charleston, which he did.

There is no way to express your feeling when a lawyer levels allegations at your husband such as "willful, wanton, gross negligence" and "gross deviation from the standard practice of medicine." After that testimony was given, I had to leave the courtroom and take a walk in City Hall Park by myself. Did I really hear those words? Was this really happening? Was all this really necessary?

The support of our twenty-two-year-old son was extremely helpful. He came to the trial and held my hand. The Sunday before the trial began, he spent the day with us – going to church, watching basketball games, going to dinner, and watching a movie. At the time, he very much wanted to go to medical school. Several times I wanted to say to him, "Don't do it, and don't put yourself and your family in a position to have to endure this."

As the trial progressed, my family felt a great need to share our experience with anyone who would listen. Gone were the first emotions of embarrassment and humiliation at being sued for malpractice. While grocery shopping, I would find myself relating the trial to mere acquaintances. I had never done anything like that before. At this time, a few of us tried valiantly to get some help with Medical Malpractice Insurance Reform, but there was apparently little continued interest from the Medical Auxiliary community.

The wife of another physician who had been sued said to me, "Martha, you will survive this, but you will never get over it." At the end of each day of trial, I would return home to days of unopened mail, unwashed clothes, and dishes that kept stacking up. I would start unloading the dishwasher and decide that it wasn't important. I was consumed by the testimony of that day. I went for four nights without sleep. Only when it was all over did I decompress and have a good cry. My mother was severely ill in intensive care at this time, and I was terribly torn in trying to spend time with her and be with my husband. I stayed with her all night – never sleeping – the morning came and I felt like I had to go be with Fletcher for a little time. He was hurting, he was to testify in court today. I was scared of the cross examining him. As I walked down the hospital corridor, I heard my mother screaming "Martha please don't leave me, I am so afraid." – I just leaned up against the hospital wall and looked up and prayed – "God, I know you told me there was not anything we could not handle together – but please help me."

My mother had a stroke soon after this and those were the last words I remember her saying. My mother was a good woman who lived an exemplary life. She did not deserver to die like that.

Was the trial really worth this?

A wonderful friend wrote a prayer for me: "I confess that I want to control my life, but daily give me the will to allow You to be in control so that I will have peace that passes all understanding and so Your spirit can dwell in me."

My husband has always been a supreme optimist, always happy and open. During this case, he became quiescent, sullen, and uncommunicative. He snapped at me for no reason. Finally, he admitted he was dealing with "controlled anger." After he gave his testimony, he went in the men's room and became physically ill. Those who practice medicine are not familiar with such an adversarial situation and language.

We reached out to our minister. He suggested Psalm 27. We were plagued with the question, "What are our true feelings for the plaintiffs and expert witness?" Of course, our first very human response, was to strike back. Did we hate them? We certainly didn't believe in "eye for an eye, a tooth for a tooth." But what do you really feel for someone who causes you such emotional trauma and grief? We searched our hearts and found that these people really had our pity and sympathy. There was no malice toward them. We grieved for an end to a friendship and trust. We truly wished them well. However, there was the knowledge that the friendship could never be rekindled. Future encounters with them and those who supported them would certainly be difficult.

We were extremely fortunate to have a brilliant, articulate lawyer. He gave us wonderful advice and kept our emotions in check. His organization and impeccable demeanor in the courtroom had to impress the jury.

The jury brought a verdict in our favor. Please note that I did not say, "We won." There were no winners that day. We were all losers. Perhaps the greatest loser was the medical profession; such a noble calling, not an exact science, but the art of helping others.

The plaintiff and his attorney took his case before the South Carolina Court of Appeals. The Court ruled there was no reason to reverse the jury decision. It agreed that the plaintiff's failure to return to his doctor for more than a year after his symptoms changed dramatically prevented his doctor from diagnosing and treating this condition. When he called my husband for pain pills, my husband was working in the garden. I usually leave the room when friends call my husband because I do not want to hear anything professional. However, this time I stayed in the room. The patient told me a joke I wanted my husband to explain to me. I heard my husband tell him, "If you are having this much pain, you should see your doctor as soon as possible." This patient waited over twelve months to do that – treating himself all the time.

What did we learn from all this? We certainly were able to endure the unthinkable with confidence in ourselves and God's help. We learned to focus our attention on things that really matter. We know our marriage was based on complete love, devotion, and commitment to each other. We never lost our pride to be members of the medical profession.

August 2004

My husband is now in his 46th year of medical practice. My son practices medicine also, I decided to print this after all these years because of two wonderful professions – law and medicine – are at odds. My sympathy certainly goes to the patient who has been involved in true malpractice. In the right circumstance, they need compensation. Our attorney asked the plaintiff why my husband was included in the case. His answer was, "I did it on the advice of my attorney." The law profession must answer to its own who bring frivolous lawsuits. I spoke to a juror after the verdict came back. He said the jury never discussed my husband's association in this case. They considered it too frivolous and insignificant to take up their time. I have never forgotten these words and wondered to this day why we had to endure this trauma.

My husband had been an expert witness in two other cases brought by the plaintiff's attorney. Will doctors be afraid to be an expert witness in the future?

When this happened, my husband already had a full load of patients and they continued to come to him. But what happens to the young doctor who is charged in a frivolous lawsuit? His or her career could be ruined. Patients who heard may stop seeing that doctor, thinking he made a terrible mistake. Other doctors may be unwilling to refer patients. The non-medical world must know exactly what a frivolous lawsuit is. I hope this will help everyone to understand one of the reasons for the high cost of medical care and malpractice insurance.

Good health care is the hope and determination for all. We must think first of the patient, but we must also remember the physician and his family. Some doctors leave the courtroom never to practice again; some practice seeing each patient as a potential plaintiff. Some keep on practicing hoping some lawyer will not see dollar signs in an unfortunate result of competent medical care. That is an absolute tragedy. Medicine is not an exact science. What happens if there are no surgeons or obstetricians to take the Hippocratic Oath? The practice of medicine should be a joy – to help others. A grateful, healthy patient is the only reason for the practice of medicine.

Each profession, law and medicine, must better monitor their own so that the two professions will not be at odds. Frivolous lawsuits, escalating premiums, and damaged reputations do not work for the welfare of the patient. This system needs fixing, and these two noble professions must seek a proper common ground. One step is the avoidance of the frivolous lawsuit.

"It takes the wisdom of Solomon to decide whether an incident was caused by negligence or was the unfortunate result of competent medical care." – *Anonymous*

Addendum

Our son admired his father's life and chose to follow him into medicine. He is now an internist. We are also proud that a granddaughter chose to become an OB-GYN working with difficult pregnancies.

A beautiful thing then happened about two years later. The plaintiff's wife saw me at a luncheon – walked across the room to me and said, "Martha, I am so sorry for the lawsuit – we should not have done it. Will you forgive me?" I reached over and gave her a big hug and said, "I love you." – And I meant it!

This appeared in the *South Carolina Medical Journal* in 1981.

HURRICANE HUGO

I sent this letter to all Urology, Army, and Washington friends.

Dear family and friends:

Do you realize that there is a new dirty 4-letter word? H U G O. Do you realize how wonderful clean clothes are? Do you realize how exhilarating a cold shower is? Do you realize how you always flip on the light when you go to the bathroom? Do you realize how exciting it is to flush the toilet? Do you realize the complications of having a new lab puppy in the midst of a hurricane? Do you realize how delicious a Hardee hamburger is? Do you realize we can't blame all of this on the Yankees?

So many of you have called and written us. We do appreciate your concern. The Derricks are all alive – well – industrious – innovative – resourceful, and optimistic about the future. However, there are moments of being overwhelmed by all our tasks. We go to bed exhausted.

We were in Europe having a great time. When we realized HUGO was really coming to Charleston, we caught the first plane and arrived right after the hurricane. We were able to ascertain that Carl was safe with the Hanckels at Coburg before boarding the plane. Loraine said she never thought she would get a phone call from Munich in the middle of a hurricane!

Of course, Carl had to secure both houses. He had great help at the beach from Emma, Wallace, Zerno, and Lynwood! We were very proud of him for all he did.

Our lovely city has been severely damaged, but not devastated. The London papers ran the headline, "Charleston – Gone with the Wind." That is definitely not true. The historic houses and buildings are still here but will require many repairs. Almost all lost roofs, or part of them. Many windows were blown out. There was much water damage. The greatest loss was all our lovely trees – just gone. They can't be replaced. We are seeing things we never saw before and sometimes get disoriented.

Mottie said coming home to 2 Gibbes was just like Scarlett coming back to Tara. She did the same thing Scarlett did – came running up the stairs screaming for her mother. 2 Gibbes lost part of the roof. It poured rain 2 days later before any repairs could be made. Everything in the attic was soaked – plaster coming down – paint peeling – air-conditioners and furnaces gone. Several windows blown out. All furniture near a window will have to be refinished. The dampness and musty odor are unbelievable. We did not have water to come into the house – it came to the next to the top step. My neighbors were not so lucky. Many of them had 5' of water in the first floor – shrimp jumping in the living room; a flounder found in a chair. Scottie had water in her kitchen drawers. All this turned to black mud – just an awful mess. Soaked oriental rugs were hung on brick walls to dry. Many of our neighbors and friends had to move out of their homes. Falling plaster made them unsafe.

The most devastation was at Sullivan's Island. Our house still stands, but with much damage. A 20' surge of water hit it. It is 18' from the ground. The floor buckled from the force of the water. Several windows and doors blew out. We lost most of the carpet, furniture, and mattresses. Everything under the house is gone – air-conditioners, boats, etc. (Carl found one of the boats 5 blocks away against a tree.) Fletcher built that house to survive a hurricane, and it did. He fired the contractor who was "jetting in" the pilings (you can only go down 12' that way). He wanted the pilings "banged in" (down to 25'). The floor joists were bolted to the pilings. Hurricane clips were put on the floor sills and rafters. I hated the beams across the cathedral ceilings – actually pouted when the architect said they had to be there to hold the house together. Of course, the fact that the house is built on a WWII gun turret helped.

Our neighbors at the beach were not so lucky. The Barrys' house on one side is gone (all that remains is a typewriter in the sand). The Self house on the other side is a shell. A tornado hit the row of houses behind us – there were 8 houses there that are now only rubble. Our house is the only livable one for about 10 blocks. It will be very sad to go back there without my neighbors.

The bridge to the Island was destroyed. They declared martial law and sent in the National Guard. Fletcher and Carl found a boat and went on the surf side; swam to shore and saw that the house was there. Carl and I went several days later on the first ferry. We were allowed to bring back only one suitcase. 120 people were on the boat; not one person shed a tear – we were all too dazed. Almost everybody lost all their possessions.

Many of you have asked how you can help. I am giving several suggestions. Please make out the check to the organization and send it to me.

Salvation Army (great job)

Interfaith Crisis Ministry (they take care of the homeless)

Sullivan's Island Relief Fund (about 50 retired couples of low and moderate incomes lost their homes).

First Baptist Church – as Chairman of Deacons, Fletcher had this responsibility also. The church lost the roof – water pouring in. The organ is gone – domed ceiling falling – carpet ruined – columns splitting and pews buckling. A disaster team from Detroit is helping with giant humidifiers. It will be very expensive.

We would certainly appreciate all you can do for our city. Economically, this is truly as disaster. The people of low income are really suffering (upper

King Street and environs were hard hit).

I recently read an account written by a Southern lady returning to Charleston after the War Between the States. She saw all the devastation. There were flowers blooming. She coined the phrase, "Flowers have no memories." As I stood in ankle-deep mud in what had been Fletcher's beloved garden, there was one rose blooming. I was furious! How dare that rose bloom in all the destruction. Then I remembered the phrase – "flowers have no memories."

SULLIVAN'S ISLAND MILITARY HISTORY

We remodeled a house at 2905 Marshall Boulevard in the 1970's. It was built on a gun turret which had a great deal to do with the house sustaining minor damage when a large portion of that area was destroyed – during hurricane Hugo.

There is much military history on the island. This part of the island was called the Marshall Military Reservation (1776-1947). During WWII, a sub post of Fort Moultrie was built upon the ruins of Revolutionary and Civil War posts. A battery was constructed there in 1776 to stop the British invasion from the Isle of Palms. The battery constructed in 1863 by Confederate troops also overlooked Breach Inlet. Those soldiers in both wars not killed by gunfire risked being drowned in the Inlet's current. In 1865, the armament consisted of heavy guns. This is the area the submersible H.L. Hunley reported departed.

During WWII, the Marshall Reservation had barracks and supported facilities of Fort Moultrie. The battery consisted of four Panama gun turrets. Four of this kind were built along the island then – ours and one in the vicinity of Station 30 that resurfaced in recent years. It appears from time to time in the erosion and accretion cycles.

A diary has been discovered of a Germany U-Boat Captain in Charleston Harbor around 1942. One U-455 managed to come within a half mile of the Charleston jetties. During the day, the boat would submerge and rest in deep water – shutting down so as not to exhaust the battery. The captain writes of spreading a dozen underwater mines around the Charleston harbor approaches in hopes of blasting a merchant ship. However, there is no record of a mine sinking a ship.

Captain Geisler tells of seeing Charleston as a bright glow on the horizon at a range of about 30 nautical miles. The arch of the Grace Bridge and the blinking harbor markings stood out.

This diary is one of our numerous reminders of the vast and interesting military history of the island. It particularly meant so very much to my husband, and he loved that gun turret.

These concrete gun turrets (Panama mounts) installed in 1942, were fitted with 155-millimeter field artillery guns. They had barrels 20 feet long and a range of over 10 miles. They were put there as Charleston's harbor defense when the United Stated officially entered the war. They were designed to defend the harbor from attacks of fast-moving torpedo boats. Two of the Panama gun mounts were transported to Folly Beach during the war according to South Carolina Department of Archives and History – so we know what happened to all four – those, ours and one that resurfaced after record high tides in 2018 near Station 30.

Bunkers were constructed during the Endicott Period (1898 – 1903). One today houses the island's Charleston County Branch Library. There are three now on the Marshall reservation – one is used as a private home – one has a home built on top. They were originally equipped with different millimeter guns and anti-aircraft guns in 1943. The guns of all the Endicott batteries were upgraded at some point between installation and WWII.

My father, James Crosson Langford – a cadet at the Citadel – was appointed 2nd lieutenant in the Coastal Artillery Company of the Army by the President of the United States on June 1, 1930. He was to report to the 534th Coastal Artillery.

He spoke often of staying at the officer's quarters on the island which were constructed from 1902 to 1930's – most likely during WWI (1914 – 1920's). These quarters are now rented as private apartments.

After our many travels, we looked forward to coming home to the serene and beautiful Sullivan's – we should all be thankful the military history there protected our city during four wars.

RETURN TO GERMANY FOR A VISIT
This previously was published in the Charleston Mercury.

My husband, Dr. Fletcher Derrick, and I, with our eighteen-year-old grandson, Ron, made a sentimental journey to Germany, where our family lived for three years, to revisit old haunts and to see the birthplace of Ron's mother.

When we were stationed at Fort Benning, we received our next assignment – Baumholder, Germany. We were thrilled until an old Army sergeant asked, "Who did that to you?" What started out to be a disaster was made something pleasant, useful, memorable, and informative. The most important event was that Mottie was born here.

Baumholder, Germany, is in the extreme southwestern part in the state of Phineland-Pfaltz. The first mention of Baumholder dates to 1156. It is near Idar-Oberstein, known for its Moselle wine and gem finishing. A former Roman outpost at Trier is also nearby.

Hitler and the Third Reich needed a training area for his panzer division. They chose Baumholder. The rumor was the Panzer division volunteered for the Russian front to get out of Baumholder.

Home to one of the largest concentrations of combat soldiers outside the United States, it consisted of Smith Barracks (the main post) and the best operations area support teams of Strassburg in Idar-Oberstein and Neubrucke, near Birkenfeld. It was a very high deployment post. Fifty percent of Baumholder units took part in the war in Kosovo. Baumholder was used for training of the fighting troops in Iraq and Afghanistan.

What was so bad about Baumholder? First, the train backed in. It is about an hour away from the Autobahn. We saw the sun about ten days out of the year. There was nothing to do. Young recruits just deployed there were lonely and depressed. Many suicides occurred, including one wife in our stairwell. Entertainment on post consisted of a PX, theatre and bowling alley. Sixty-two bars were in the small town. Although prostitution was illegal until 2003, most of the bars had some sort of arrangement with the maids. One day after we arrived in Baumholder, I looked out the window and a cattle truck came by loaded with women dressed in fancy clothes. Fletcher later told me it was pay day in Baumholder, and the truck went around the village gathering women for the bars. I had never seen such a thing! The young American wives found themselves without an outlet; living on the "economy" instead of post housing sometimes meant the shoveling of coal to keep the furnaces going and to stay warm. This was true for the "Cold War" and is fifty years later for the war in which we now find ourselves.

Today, Landstuhl is an important part of our lives. The wounded from the eastern wars are stabilized, flown to Ramstein Air Base just down the hill, brought to Landstuhl for definitive surgery and further stabilization and air evacuation to a hospital near their home in the USA. A doctor and/or nurse usually accompanies the seriously injured patients – Fletcher made many such trips. Much of the air evacuation is provided by the C-17 Wings at Charleston Air Base.

Fletcher and Ron found appropriated some 29,158 acres to be used for combat training, and the outdoor training, and the outdoor firing ranges afforded this with ease.

So how did we handle that year? Knowing no one, I learned to knock on the neighbors' doors and invite them for a cup of coffee. I met some wonderful people that way. Of course, without TV, I read nearly every book in the Special Services Library. Luckily, I took up duplicate bridge and learned to drive all over Germany going antique shopping. I spent some time with our chaplain helping refugees from East Germany (before the wall). The men were in the field training so much of the time that some outlet had to be found.

Fletcher was the surgeon for the 8th Division Artillery. Having gone to Clemson during the days of the cadet corps, he adjusted quickly to maneuvers and field medicine surgery. Although Baumholder had medical clinics, thirty minutes away was an acute care hospital which was primarily for military, but also served dependents at that time. Our daughter was born there. It was built on the main military railroad from Frankfurt to Paris. The railroad's sole purpose was for military operations. It had a vital position in case the Cold War became "hot."

Our next appointment was to Landstuhl Army Hospital, about an hour from Baumholder and the army medical center for Europe, with all medical specialists represented. The commander at that time was Colonel Fred

Knobeloch from Charleston, a graduate of the Medical University of South Carolina. When Fletcher called on the commanding officer, he learned that Colonel Knobeloch was also a Citadel graduate and a classmate of my father.

The only picture of Carl with his Derrick grandfather.

With German friends Gretchen and Verner.

Irma – a wonderful German "Nanny".

Carl at Nixon inauguration.

Mottie at Clemson.

At Nixon's Inauguration.

Mottie planning a fashion show.

Mottie's debut with Carl.

Ashley Hall graduate.

Debut in New York.

Mottie and Paul wedding picture.

Carl and Melissa.

Graduation from Porter-Gaud with both Grandmothers.

Carl and boys at wedding.

Carl with old friends.

Carl, Melissa, Gaby.

Melissa's wedding picture.

Gaby's debut in Beaufort.

Paul and Owen.

Paul and Derrick.

With Hanckels and "other Mother".

KILIMANJARO "THE ROOF OF AFRICA"

This appeared in The Mercury.

Fletcher had always been an excellent athlete. He played football and basketball in high school. His mother said she went to football games just to see if number 21 got up. During his medical training there was little time to be athletic. So, we followed the Clemson football and our annual spring break with the children was when we went to the ACC basketball tournaments – usually in Greensboro. All those games were for four days. Carl and Mottie always looked forward to that.

Fletcher's father was one of nine brothers. All died of heart disease – so Fletcher started jogging when we lived in Washington. When he was about sixty years old, he announced he was going to climb Kilimanjaro in East Africa. I was not at all familiar with this – but if he wanted to do it, I supported him.

He started rigorous training – particularly running up the stairs in parking garages – sometimes with weights strapped on his legs. Mottie called me one day and said, "Mom, you have got to stop Dad from running all over the city in those horrible clothes. It is embarrassing." Then one day I came home to find something on my piazza that looked like a small refrigerator. He had ordered a machine from Australia to help him breathe in low oxygen.

The mountain was 19,340 ft. climb. He sat the machine up in his study and stayed there every night. I and the dog (Claudette) sat with him often. I was ready for our next trip. When he finished with the machine, he sent it to Hilton Head where it was used for people to ski in North Carolina.

He and our son Carl – who was a physician also – were walking over to the Hibernian Hall for a meeting. Fletcher just happened to mention to him that when he did very strenuous exercises a persistent and mysterious place in the back of his neck was painful. Carl said, "Dad, you need a heart cath." The subsequent tests revealed a 70 percent blockage in three of his arteries and a fourth showed a blockage of 90 percent in his neck. He underwent open heart surgery. Of course, the trip was cancelled – yet about six months later the adventure was back on the calendar. People asked me why I didn't try to stop this. The reason being, I married Fletcher Derrick to share his life, not to run it. I knew how much this meant to him.

Throughout our married life I was offered jobs and positions in Charleston and South Carolina. I almost have two degrees in business administration and history, but I chose to spend my time helping him in his career and being there when he needed me.

We had such a close relationship he wanted me to be nearby when he was home - even if he was just taking a snooze. I did manage to be a trustee for two South Carolina nursing homes and a trustee at Coker College.

Major Riley appointed me to the city's tourism commission. Since I was a city guide, I really enjoyed this. I helped to write the guide notes to be studied for the exam – lectured to the potential guides, wrote the exam, and administered it.

I still believe if it had not been for this quest and the extensive training it required, he may have never felt the warning signs. The trip may have saved his life.

He was the oldest man on the trek, and they asked him to give a pep talk the night before they climbed. They let him reach the summit first, and he pulled a number all the way up. A friend shouted, "Meet you at the top." Then when Fletcher died years later, there was a family visitation before the funeral. This friend wrote in the book - "Meet you at the top." That is how the title of this book came to be.

I was standing there when he came down.

We then went on a safari in Tanzania.

PHYSICIAN CLIMBS MT. KILIMANJARO FOLLOWING QUADRUPLE BYPASS

This appeared in the Journal of the South Carolina Medical Association

Urologist Fletcher Derrick, MD, of Roper Hospital made his way to "The Roof of Africa" in early August 2003, a mere year and a half after cardiologists performed a quadruple bypass on the seventy-year-old physician.

Derrick was originally scheduled to climb Mt. Kilimanjaro in 2002. But as his training schedule intensified, so did his persistent – and mysterious – neck pain, until ultimately it led him to his physician. Subsequent tests revealed 70 percent blockages in three of his arteries. A fourth showed a blockage of 90 percent.

The trip was postponed. On March 14, 2002, Derrick underwent open heart surgery at Roper Hospital. Yet only six months later, the African adventure was back on the calendar, and the former army medic resumed a training schedule that included backpacking, bicycling, and low-oxygen training.

In August 2003, he joined twelve fellow trekkers and set out for the 19,340-foot Tanzanian climb, on his way to Uhuru, Mt. Kilimanjaro's highest peak.

Yet it was only after he led his group to the top that Derrick confided to his fellow climbers that for him, the voyage had begun eighteen months earlier, on the operating table to clear four blocked arteries. The group was stunned.

According to his wife, Martha, had it not been for this quest and extensive training it required, he may never have felt the warning signs. As for Derrick himself, this journey was a very special challenge – one that may even have saved his life.

TANZANIA

I left Charleston for Africa a week after Fletcher. My first destination was Amsterdam. I asked my travel agent for a five-star hotel near the Rembrandt Exhibit.

I knew Fletcher would call me at my hotel.

Now the wait – I was extremely nervous. I called Mottie and Loraine, and they calmed me down. I had trouble calling on the phone with eight digits. Later Fletcher told me I had evidently new friends in Poland and one in New Mexico.

Then he called, he had made it! The other climbers let him go up first. Then he was able to pull up some who were having trouble at the last. He didn't stay up long. There was a thirty-mile-an-hour wind.

The next day I had a very enjoyable flight down the center of Africa. Kenya was having some trouble, so we travelled to avoid going near there.

I was there when Fletcher came down with open arms, and we had a wonderful reunion. I enjoyed meeting others on the trip, as well.

Then we started our safari of Tanzania and the Serengeti Olduvai Gorge. Thomson's Safaris had planned everything for us, and it was executed beautifully. We were there for about two weeks. We spent several nights in some small huts and some in tents in the wild. We had a bucket of water for a shower for two. The grass had been cut from about three feet from our tent and a man with a gun stood there all night.

One night we didn't get much sleep. The other group of younger folks had too much to drink. There were several big bonfires so there was plenty of light. They took turns running into the grass and seeing who had the nerve to stay there the longest. The lions and the hyenas were the most dangerous. They could be noisy at times.

How majestic it was to see the lovely animals that hopped in their native habitat. The Dik-Diks (a species of antelope) were my favorite – such small animals. We saw many leopards sleeping in trees with their legs hanging down, to be safe from other predators. One day we drove up to a tree and under it was a pride of lions, mother, father, and cubs. Fletcher took pictures and painted them later. I loved watching the giraffe drink. The only way a lion could kill him was to grab at the neck. So, the giraffe looked up, down, right, and left before putting his head down to drink.

After these wonderful scenes we had to head back to civilization. We had gone so far into the bush that we had to fly back in a small plane to our hotel. There were some souvenir shops there where Fletcher bought me a small tanzanite.

Our trip home was comfortable, but we were so glad we had seen those African sunsets and majestic animals.

THE LEAKEYS

One of the highlights of the Tanzania trip was really to stand where the Leakeys lived and worked. The Leakeys were a Kenyan-British family of paleoanthropologists who made important discoveries related to the origin of humankind. The Olduvai Gorge, in northern Tanzania, was where some of the earliest evidence of mankind was found, and the museum there was founded by Mary Leakey (1913-1996), wife of Louis Leakey (1903-1972).

This was wonderful for Fletcher. He had admired their work for a long time.

I was frustrated by the visit here. It was too short! I wanted to hear more about the history of their work – and explore the museum where there was a picture of the first child's footprint ever found in the Olduvai Gorge. I also wanted to purchase some of the jewelry they made there.

The Leakeys were early in their beliefs about early man. "I believe in Darwin's theory that the mystery of man's past would be unraveled here in Africa," wrote Louis Leakey. "I am convinced that Africa, not Asia, is the cradle of mankind." Their family is still involved in paleoanthropological research in East Africa.

The Olduvai Gorge and the Serengeti Plain are major attractions in Tanzania largely due to the renown of the Leakeys. Their contact with the Masai indigenous people aided the family in their discoveries. The Masai people were congenial and helpful to them.

CHRISTMAS IN INDOCHINA

This appeared in The Mercury.

Christmas in Indochina? My aunt shook her head and told me she didn't know anybody who would do such a thing. But now she does. My husband, Fletcher, and I spent the holidays in Vietnam.

Both of us have strong interest in learning about other cultures. Fletcher loves geography and history is my specialty. We also love adventure, all of which made for a trip of a lifetime. We flew to Saigon via Bangkok, Thailand – a 22-hour trip from Charleston. Once in Saigon, we soon took a tour of the city's version of China Town. The Vietnamese guide wasted no time in saying, with obvious disdain, that the Chinese were dirty and noisy.

Saigon itself was relatively clean and bustling. Quite to our surprise, it was engaged in what might be described as the Christmas spirit. The Christmas tree in the lobby of the Sheraton Hotel where we stayed was a pleasant surprise. The tree was at least 30 feet tall and the decorations were the most beautiful we had ever seen. Most of the ornaments were flowers of gold, red, and white. White orchids hung like banners entwined with silver throughout the hotel.

Elsewhere in the city, storefronts were lit up by similar décor. Outside one of the hotels, lighted garlands stretched from window to window, and trees around an outdoor pool were laden with lights that were beautifully reflected in the water below. But the spirit was strictly commercial – "Jingle Bells" filled the elevator but no renditions of "O Holy Night" were anywhere to be found.

The following morning Fletcher and our guide went to the Viet Cong Tunnels of Cu Chi. A documentary film was shown there which lauded the men and women who used the secret tunnels in their fight. Fletcher learned how booby traps were constructed and camouflaged. Some of the tunnels were quite small, which was suitable for most Vietnamese, but difficult for larger Westerners such as Fletcher. One tunnel required that he crawl about 50 feet on hands and knees before entering a small dining room and medical area. There were air vents made of bamboo all along the way.

When South Vietnam fell, some of its leaders thought they might have a say in the new government. But until about 1985, the communists arrested many who helped the Americans and sent them to "re-education camps" never to be seen again. Today, there is a degree of freedom for citizens to come and go almost anywhere except the United States. It is hard to get a visa, which costs about $200 and requires the applicant to pass a written exam. The authorities seem only to give visas to the older Vietnamese, who they are confident will return.

Generally, the people seemed happy. But we were tourists and local guides were careful about where they took us. Although the government is communist, some commercialism is allowed.

We were taken to a Gothic cathedral called Notre Dame, built around 1880. Its rose window was covered, but the remainder of the building was like others around the world. There was a large statue of Mary that, to some viewers, appeared to shed tears. Many pilgrims were worshipping in the cathedral in front of the statue when we were there. Vietnam is about 12 percent Christian (mostly Catholics) and 88 percent Buddhist.

The city's air was horribly polluted, and people wore masks to protect their lungs. Many women also wore long white gloves to protect their skin. Nine million people live in Saigon and own an estimated 2.5 million motor scooters and 3 million bikes.

Our guide and I went antique shopping one day. As we crossed the street, the guide said, "Hold my hand Madame, walk slowly, and please under no condition stop walking." The drivers of the scooters zipped by right and left as we crossed the avenue, and once we made it, I vowed never to try it again. However, I bought a lovely piece of china from the China Sea.

The resort town of DaNang is lovely. It had been a rest area for American military personnel during the war. But the place was almost vacant when we went there because of a small hurricane in the vicinity. The surfers at Folly Beach would have had a wonderful time, but we learned later that thirty-four people had drowned during the passing of the storm.

Fletcher went to the ancient port city of Hoi An. It is only for pedestrians and has much Chinese influence. Nonetheless, there were Christmas decorations there too. This city is one big market because it lies on one of Vietnam's main rivers, the Thu Bon. Many people come down to Hoi An from the hill country to sell their wares, which include pottery, jade and silk. Several ornate Buddhist temples are located there, too.

When we arrived in Hanoi, the first thing we were told was not to eat the chicken or the eggs because of the threat of the deadly avian flu. Our hotel was very French. Hanoi is situated on a low ground along the Red River and many dikes protect it. We took a ride on a pedicab through the oldest district. While on the pedicab we saw numerous signs of modern commerce, with streets lined with stores selling everything imaginable. There was a shoe district, a clothing district, an ornament district, an art district, etc. Most of the merchants live over their stores.

Just outside the city is what is known as the "ghost market." Flower and produce growers take their harvests there around midnight and leave around 6:00 a.m. Retailers buy from them at night in preparation for the coming day.

The country around Hanoi is mostly mountainous. We took a helicopter trip to Halong where a new bridge and harbor were under construction. We saw many ships laden with coal and other ore from the area. Being in the North near China, this region has seen many wars, and animosity still runs high. Oil had recently been discovered just off the shore and the Vietnamese were working day and night to get the wells up and running.

All in all, the people were pleasant and displayed no animosity to Americans. I asked our guide if he thought the United State could have won the war, and he said, "Madam, I have not been asked that question since 1997, and the answer is no." The people were fighting for their homeland, he explained. The tunnels, jungles and mountains made war very difficult for the Americans. A platoon might walk through men gathering rice, pass by them, and they might turn and open fire. There was no way to know who the enemy was, he said.

Vietnam became a part of Indochina in 1884 and continued so until 1954 when the communists, under Ho Chi Minh, took power and wars with France and the United States followed. There was a very conservative communist rule until around 2001 when the economy began to get more competitive. Tourists are welcomed in Vietnam today.

On our tour of Hanoi, Fletcher visited the "Hanoi Hilton," a former prison camp of US captives. Pictures of US Sen. John McCain and other pilots are prominently displayed on the wall of the old prison. The people of Vietnam admire McCain. When his plane went down, he parachuted into the middle of a lake in front of Ho Chi Minh's home. McCain was offered his freedom when his captors learned that his father was a high-ranking US admiral. But John McCain responded that he would not leave without the other US captives and remained a prisoner there for seven years.

The tomb and home of Ho Chi Minh are very simple. We also visited the Van Mieu Temple, an education center nearby that has promoted the teachings of Confucius since 1070 A.D. Vietnamese people think of Confucius' teachings as a kind of etiquette one should use for life. Today they also have a strong belief in the Buddha to absolve themselves of sin.

We went to Halong Bay and took a boat trip around the Emerald Isles – a very unusual land formation of volcanic rock. Fletcher visited a grotto there. The islands are uninhabited except for birds and a few monkeys. The water is beautiful and "fish farming" is conducted from houseboats.

We left Hanoi with positive feelings for the people of Vietnam and their future. We are aware that on a tour we saw only what the authorities wanted us to see; however, someday the country might become more open.

SOUTH AFRICA

Africa seemed to call to us. We had been there four times and still wanted to return. This time we wanted to study the life of Nelson Mandela and his association with the French Huguenot F.W. de Klerk.

The revocation of the Edict of Nantes in 1685 by King Louis XIV left the Huguenots few choices. Some chose to revert to Catholicism. Some worshipped in secrecy and many left France – leaving everything behind. Several places offered freedom of worship: The Netherlands, England, Germany, Switzerland, English and Dutch colonies in America and the Cape Colony, a Dutch holding at the Cape of Good Hope in South Africa

The first group of Huguenot immigrants to the Cape Colony left the Netherlands in 1687 and had a very difficult voyage down the west coast of Africa. The ships were small and there was much disease and hunger. When they arrived, they were met by white farmers and the Hottentots. The Hottentots gave some help.

Farms were given freely to the immigrants by Dutch authorities. The Huguenots received some financial assistance from the Dutch East India Company. They gave them food, building products and wagons. They had to fight the unpredictable weather (droughts and plagues) and some wild animals. By 1729 the number of Huguenots at the Cape was 279.

The bay was known to sailors as a safe refuge at sea and a convenient place where damaged ships could be repaired. This increased trade with eastern places.

The Huguenots gradually adapted to the new environment. They were good workers and made a significant contribution to civil life. They stayed close to the teachings of Calvin.

Vineyards and wheat farming were the two important branches of agriculture at the Cape and the Huguenots who had been involved in these activities in France knew how to grow both. They reinforced the efforts of Cape colonists who had been farming before the Huguenots arrived. Wine experts also came to the Cape. It was a long struggle to make it a good wine that could compete with the European wines.

About Nelson Mandela – we visited Robben Island where he was imprisoned for many years. When he was released, he wasn't bitter, nor sought revenge. Mandela was the most famous political prisoner in the world.

De Klerk, the state president of the Union of South Africa, 1989-94, for a long time had been associated with his country's racist apartheid government. The two men met and were able to avoid a possible civil war and achieve a free South Africa. They shared the Noble Prize for Peace that year, 1993.

Frederik Willem de Klerk's tenth great-grandfather, Étienne le Clercq, was a French Huguenot immigrant.

After exploring the Cape of Good Hope, we went on a safari in northern South Africa and were able to see the Victoria Falls, on the border between Zambia and Zimbabwe. The falls were named in 1855 by the Scots missionary David Livingston, in honor of his sovereign, Queen Victoria.

NIGERIA

After leading a seminar of army urologists in Nuremburg, Germany, Fletcher and the family spent several weeks in Ogbomosho, Nigeria, working in the Southern Baptist Hospital under the auspicious of the Foreign Mission Board. Ogbomosho is a city of about 350,000 people. Baptist missionaries have been there since 1855. There is the hospital and the Nigeria Baptist Seminary.

The Southern Baptist Hospital is a large facility where they train interns and residents and they never had had a urologist there – so Fletcher was welcomed to teach urological surgery. Fletcher gave lectures to the Nigerian interns and residents. He spent most of his day in surgery. The hospital had been saving certain urological cases for him.

Fletcher had wanted to go on a medical mission trip to Africa for a long time. Finding just the right place for the trip to use his specialty was difficult. We were lucky to have a missionary nurse friend direct us to the Southern Baptist Hospital in Ogbomosho.

The Ogbomosho area's economy is mainly agricultural. There is no industry, few stores, and few ways to make a living. Commerce is done by bartering on the street whatever you have to sell. Poverty is all around – as is illness.

There are many American missionary guests from different Christian denominations. The hospital has a guest house for patients to stay when they come to see a special doctor. That is also where we stayed with our children, Mottie (then 16) and Carl (10).

The missionary children went to school in Jos, in north central Nigeria, and did not come home until the summer. They were delighted to have new playmates. The teenage boys thought our blonde pretty daughter was wonderful. As we left weeks later, they followed us on their motorcycles. The next time the family had leave to come to the States, the whole family were our house guests.

Getting in and out of Africa was difficult. The Nigerian airline had two planes, and they were often in need of repair and where was that – as for anything else – Germany period. We learned not to fly Nigerian planes.

We spent several days in Europe ending up in Italy to take the Nigerian flight. We left for Africa at midnight – walking to the plane escorted by men with machine guns.

Arriving in Lagos was a mob scene. Africans apparently don't know what queue means. They don't know how to stand in line. In the midst of this, we looked up and saw a familiar face – Dr. Erete Amaku – who was a urologist at the University of Lagos. He had been on programs with Fletcher in the States. He took us under his care and got us through customs.

Then we had to get to our hotel. There are one million people in Lagos and (apparently) one stoplight. About an hour later we arrived at a hotel that was not a four-star hotel. I tried to contact our parents in the states to tell them we were safe in Africa. We were in Nigeria for several weeks and I was never able to make that call or send a telegram.

That night we had dinner with the Amaku family. Erete's wife was an English physician. She warned us we were not taking strong enough medicine for malaria and gave us what we needed. Carl had fun playing with their small boy. We had our first Nigerian meal which always consisted of tough chicken. We taught the children to stir up their plates to make it look like they had eaten.

The next day we went to the airport to get to the interior of the country. Information said the cloud ceiling was low – so we waited several hours.

There was a one-room airport with one very slow fan. The children and I played many games of cards.

Suddenly Carl come running – "Dad has been arrested." We immediately saw two Nigerian soldiers with guns in Fletcher's back. It seems he had taken a picture of a military installation. What do we do now? Then we saw a tall Nigerian -- almost seven feet tall -- dressed all in white. He told the soldiers, "Let this man go, he has come to help us." They did, and we all breathed easily and then looked around to thank the man. He was nowhere to be found – not in the airport – not in the men's room – not in the cars or planes – nowhere. He had vanished. Our family will always think of him as our angel.

Finally, we arrived in Ogbomosho after a harrowing car drive over awful roads.

Life settled down for us. Fletcher was busy operating and teaching. One of the main physical problems was little girls trying to give birth before their bodies were equipped to do so. There were many C-sections. Then there were numerous motorcycle accidents because of no speed limits and those bad roads. It is said that the first thing that a Nigerian buys is a mattress – then a motorcycle. However, Fletcher felt his time well spent.

The hostess of the guest house suggested Mottie and I take a small trip with her. She took us to a long building with one middle entrance. Our eyes became acclimated to the darkness. There were many women lying on pieces of cloth with babies beside them. Suddenly a woman walked up to me and handed me her baby. He was covered with sores – oozing puss, no diaper and a foaming nose and mouth. I had to take the baby. What do I do? I swayed the baby back and forth and sang a hymn to him. Then I gave him back to the mother. She started laughing and crying. I asked what was wrong. I was told she had prayed that a white woman would come and hold her baby and then he would get well. Mottie and I were silent.

We attended the church service for the Nigerian Baptists and the one for the missionaries where Fletcher sang a solo. We were really scrutinized with our blonde hair and white skin. They called us "the peeled ones."

At the end of our stay, our adventurous flight out. We had to spend the night in a room over the goat market -- yuck. The children slept on chairs.

We were scheduled to leave in Nigerian planes and wanted to avoid that. I got in one line for Zurich with Mottie. Fletcher got in the line for England with Carl. We just wanted to find the quickest way to get off the continent of Africa. The Swiss man was so good-looking, I didn't know whether to cry or to proposition him. I decided to cry, and he gave us tickets on his nice clean air-conditioned plane.

We will never forget our trip to Nigeria. Erete comes to visit us when he is in the States.

Crosson and Derrick playing ball..

Martha and Fletcher celebrate a birthday.

Carl, Fletcher, Martha, Mottie at 2 Gibbes Street.

Carl's 3 – Heyward, Crosson, Stuart.

Fletcher retires – Ron, Stuart, Heyward.

All grandkids in mountains.

Planting a tree at Coker in Lois' memory.

In Carl's wedding with Martha, Eliza and Mottie.

Eliza and Ron selling lemonade to tourists.

Paul teaching Eliza to shag.

Eliza zip-lining in Costa Rica jungle.

Eliza, Weezie, Tripp.

Eliza's graduation from medical school (3 generations).

Eliza and Tripp wedding.

Eliza's debut in Charleston.

Ron at Sullivan's Island.

Ron (6 mos.), Eliza (3 years).

Martha with Katherine and Don Riopel.

Martha and Ron at Carl's wedding.

Ron and cousins.

Ron at Florence debute.

NEPAL

It was a cold and rainy night in Charleston, and all I wanted to do was relax and sit in front of the fire. Fletcher had other plans. He wanted to go to a party to which we had been invited and we went. As we walked in, Fletcher spied someone across the room. They gave each other a bear hug welcome. It was Dr. Thomas Lucas who was our State Department's Physician Director in Southeast Asia. Fletcher was so glad to see him – especially when he said you must come to Nepal and lecture and teach some surgery. Now I was very interested. It sounded too good to be true and we went and stayed as Tommy and Georgia Lucas' house guests.

What gracious hosts they were. Also spending time with them were Rick and Annie Belser from St. Michaels Church. The five of us explored almost all of Nepal. With Georgia Lucas driving on awful roads, we set out one week to find the birthplace of Buddha "the enlightened". There is in Lumbini the ruins of a castle where he was born. As a human being he lived probably between 560-480 BC in the northeastern part of India. Buddhism believes in reincarnation – he didn't come into the world the first time in 560 BC. He had undergone many births – had experienced the world as an animal, a man and as a God. During his many rebirths he would have shed the common fate of all these lives. A spiritual perfection like that as a Buddhist cannot result from just one lifetime. Nirvana was thought to be the extension of desired individual conscientiousness – bliss and heaven. The core of the movement consists of monks – they live a monastic life and live as hermits in solitude. Poverty, celibacy, and inoffensiveness are the three essentials of monastic life. Gaining Nirvana is important.

Buddhism appeals to some of our young people, who come to Nepal to trek. Pokhara is the staging area for the treks. Fletcher and I decided not to try the trail because of his knee and my back. Pokhara has businesses offering minutes to call home for the young people.

Fletcher and I spied a sign for the Pokhara Baptist Church which happened to be held at the exact time we read it. We climbed a concrete wall and walked into a huge building that had only one exit. There was no light. Our eyes became acclimated, and we saw Nepalis sitting on the floor with their

Bibles. Written on the walls was. "Peace, I leave with you, my Peace I give unto you not as the world giveth I unto you, Let not your heart be troubled neither let it be afraid" (John 14:27).

The pastor was a young Nepali and he welcomed us. We had to sit on the floor. He preached in English, then in Nepali. Only Nepalis can preach Christianity; outsiders cannot. After the service, we were invited into his office where they wanted our names and address. We corresponded with him and supported him until one day he wanted us to buy him a motorcycle. We did not do that, but we supported the United Missions of Nepal for a long time.

We had a great adventure awaiting us. When we crossed a very wide river in southern Nepal, we found ourselves in the Nepal jungle. We were informed we were going to hunt tigers or elephants. I didn't go the first time but decided to take a walk along a jungle path. I needed to be alone and meditate (five of us had been in a car for over a week). A young Nepali kept following me. Finally, I asked him to leave me alone. He said, "No madam – tigers." I started immediately back to my bungalow. It was built on stilts and at the bottom of the stairs was a small tent where Nepali guards slept with a gun. We had hot water about fifteen minutes a day – a quick shower for two people. I went to bed first, then I screamed when I thought there was some sort of animal in my bed, but it was a hot water bottle at my feet.

The next day, I rode on the elephant with Fletcher – what fun. We sat back-to-back on the elephant and the Nepali handler drove the elephant with his feet. He had a long stick. When he came near a tree branch or high grass, he would tap with his stick, and we would know to duck. There were no tigers around, maybe because the grass was burned recently.

That night they had a delicious buffet for us. What were we eating? (Two of us came home with problems). Then we sat around a huge fire in a stone pit – the fellowship and conversations were great. When we left the fire, a Nepali followed us to our bungalow. As we left to cross the river the next day and go back to civilization, it was so sad. The jungle had exceeded all our expectations. We traveled upstream in our canoe and then crossed the river at a certain spot to find the landing. A huge crocodile was standing on a rock – just like he was waiting for us.

When we left the jungle, we headed for a range of mountains to Tansen. Robert Fleming, an American ornithologist, came to Nepal in 1949 to study the country's birds. Nepal was closed to foreign missionaries; however, Fleming became aware that a medical mission would be welcomed. He returned in 1954 with his physician wife Dr. Bethel Harris Fleming and she opened a clinic in the little village. She was so welcomed that eventually a hospital was built on top of the mountain at Tansen. Fletcher visited the hospital and the surgery that was done there. That hospital was the beginning of the United Mission of Nepal, which is a thriving organization, representing Christian groups throughout the world.

We witnessed a cremation. There is a building where they go and wait to die, something like a hospice house here. We witnessed the platform next to the river where the body is lain, and wood is placed all around. Something is put over the face so it can burn first. Then the ashes are dispersed in the river.

We came back to Katmandu and had a lovely walk through Bhakpapur - a medieval section of the city. The Buddhist temples were very interesting. There were many swastikas around. We think of Hitler and the swastika. The swastika is really a symbol of the most sacred and has been used for 8,000 years. It has been the mark of the Aryan (Hindu) civilization and culture. All the Aryan scripts -- Sanskrit – Pali --Tibetan – Burmese – Siamese – Sinhalese – Roman and Latin, etc. are believed to have originated from this very symbol – the swastika. It symbolizes success, accomplishment, and perfection in every walk of like under the guidance of the Almighty. It is found not only in India, but in many other countries.

The temple also had different kinds of sex portrayed – some homosexuality.

Buddha was a Hindu prince and never said he was God. He left his wealthy family to meditate and come closer to Nirvana which was an ideal place of peace and tranquility. There was no savior, no creator God, and no hope, nothing that would be very fulfilling, to me personally.

Our time in Nepal was interesting, to see another culture, but we left with a new commitment to our faith. Christianity gives us so many things: a living father God, who wants the best for us and promises eternal life. I know I will be with Fletcher again. Jesus has left us the Bible with which to guide our lives. What a pleasure that is. Our hearts sing with love and praise for Him. Amen!

ARGENTINA

One of Fletcher's residents at George Washington University Medical Center went to Sloan Kettering Allied Memorial Hospital in New York for a one-year cancer fellowship. He was invited to stay on the faculty, had an illustrious career, and was elected President of the New York Section of the American Urological Association for 2007 and 2008. He invited us to go to the annual meeting which was held in Buenos Aires in conjunction with the Argentine Urological Society, and Fletcher was asked to be on the program.

While Fletcher was in the medical meeting, I decided to explore Buenos Aires. First, I visited the grave of Eva Peron. It was simpler than I had imagined, but in a lovely cemetery – a man and a woman were dancing the tango. It is a dance originally started for two men. It was beautifully done, and I was glad to be able to see it up close.

There were several things that were bargains in the shops. I bought leather purses for Christmas presents. Many English people went to Argentina in the 18th and 19th centuries to raise cattle and horses. When they left to return to England, they left some of their beautiful pieces of china behind. I was able to buy some.

We enjoyed the medical farewell banquet. This was a very small banquet (80 people) consisting mostly of presidents of each Argentine state's urological society. After dinner, things became very quiet. There was no announcement. Suddenly a woman appeared on the stage looking just like Eva Peron – long blonde hair pulled back in a bun and a pink net strapless dress. She sang "Don't Cry for Me Argentina" *a cappella* – so beautiful – and she quietly walked out of the room. There was no applause – we were mesmerized.

ANTARCTICA, EARTH'S LAST WILDERNESS
"End of the world and the beginning of everything"
This appeared in The Mercury.

Since we were in the neighborhood and would never be here again, we began to explore other possible destinations. Fletcher very much wanted to see Iguaçu Falls on the southern border of Brazil, where we saw the largest collection of waterfalls in our world – a tropical rainforest. These falls are about twelve times the size of Niagara.

Leaving that tropical atmosphere, we arrived five hours later in a snowstorm in Ushuaia on the way to the Drake Passage. Said to be the world's most southernmost city, it is a small town off the southern tip of Argentina where ships come before they round Cape Horn. (We saw the Horn but did not visit it). There were three ships in the harbor in Ushuaia - two brightly shining large ones and a small 300-foot Russian icebreaker which sorely needed painting. When I learned that this was our ship, my heart sank. Are we really going to do this on <u>that</u> ship? We were very glad later to be on a small ship because we were the only ones to be able to go in remote regions of icebergs and step foot on Antarctica.

When we suggested to our travel agent that we really wanted to go to Antarctica, she looked perplexed, but was able to find us the Russian icebreaker, whose schedule fit ours. The ship was the *Orlova,* of the Quark Expeditions which brings travelers to the North and South Poles. Exploring Antarctica on the ship was one of the greatest experiences of our lives. This agile, ice-strengthened ship gave us exclusive access to the peninsula's nooks and crannies. With only 90 aboard, we could see more of the continent. We found out later that the double hull reinforced us against the icebergs. The water temperature was 28 degrees Fahrenheit and would kill a human in about 2 minutes – the coldest water on Earth.

The Russian crew was hardly visible. Fletcher did go up on the bridge and observed the very experienced captain dodge icebergs that were all around us. The expedition team was made up of mostly Australians and Americans. The surroundings were pleasant, but certainly not a five-star hotel. The manager of the dining room was German. We had young beautiful Russian girls as servers.

After we boarded, we assembled and were told that we were about to cross the most treacherous and turbulent waters on our planet – the Southern Ocean where the Atlantic and Pacific Oceans come together. Not only that, but we were also headed into a storm.

It takes two days to cross the Drake Passage. We were never sick but queasy. The captain asked us please not to go to the observation bridge to not impede his vision in tight areas invisible to radar. One day the captain told us to stay in our cabin and they would bring us food and drink. We literally crawled around our cabin. The winds were 50 mph, and the waves were 30 feet. I could not look out the cabin porthole at the sea, but Fletcher did. Fletcher came to me in our bunk. I think he thought if we were going to die, we were going to die together.

The next day was Thanksgiving – my birthday. The chef of the dining room baked me a cake. I could only look at it. The next day I was able actually to eat a piece. I looked up and four Chinese were taking pictures of this old lady eating her cake. What were they going to do with that picture? Everyone sang me a "rolling birthday."

Before this the captain had come on the intercom and told us another ship like ours had hit an iceberg and was sinking. The "law" of the sea was that our ship should turn and go to the rescue. Fletcher and I went up to send a message to our family that it was not our ship. The Russian operator told us he was not able to communicate, that he had to wait for the satellite to come around. So, we waited. Finally, we were able to talk to our family and a friend. The friend said, "Martha, we are watching it now on CNN!" The ship did sink, but all passengers were saved.

This is for adventurous travelers who want to study the extreme corners of the earth – unique, beautiful, majestic, no place on earth like this. It is remote and the last known continent – a mountain of rock, 140 million years old. It is the essence of adventure – a special place in our imagination. There are 200 species of fish in the Antarctic waters – many varieties. The krill is the prey of fish, birds, and great whales. The total weight of the world's oceans is probably more than that of the human race.

The next day the sea was much calmer. We crossed the Antarctic Circle and were now in the Antarctic waters. This day we made our first stop. It was too cold and blustery, so Fletcher didn't go. The object of this tour was to see the different birds. There were lovely black ones with white spots.

Penguins' ancestors may have been flying birds, but penguins now fly underwater. Their wings are stiff and flat, and they paddle with their feet. We spent one day watching them. There were thousands of them. They aren't the pleasant creatures we see in movies. They "whack-whack," and we were informed not to go within five feet of them. They gather at the water to eat the krill.

Lying back on an iceberg, a huge seal was just waiting. It seems the penguins eat in a group thinking that gives better protection from the seal.

I found a notebook of Charles Darwin (1836-1844) where he describes the penguin as the "most-curious bird" – he thought they were associated with ducks with a long tail. He spoke of the vigor of their propelling powers; they fly rapidly underwater while flapping their wings. The penguin lays a single egg; both male and female sit on it in rookeries. It may be the most primitive of birds.

There are seals that weigh 1400 pounds that must be the most unattractive of God's creatures – huge blubber was all we saw. They swim with great speed and are solitary animals; you rarely see more than one.

We had a marvelous day. I have back problems and the last thing my neurosurgeon said to me was "Don't get in the Zodiac." But Fletcher came back to the cabin for me and helped me dress in all my paraphernalia. Going down the gangplank I was really scared, but someone yelled "special person coming" and two Russian crewmen picked me up and placed me in the Zodiac which was very stable. Everyone cheered!

I then saw the most beautiful sight I have ever seen. During the night the ship had come into a large cove. We were surrounded by icebergs as tall as a building. The water was blue-sky blue. Now I know what "iceberg blue" is. Someone asked me what you do in Antarctica – you look at icebergs. They were so magnificent. I just stared at them for hours. To think that God made this beautiful environment and man has never touched it. The experience was one of awe, and I am thankful that I was able to witness such a sight.

A geologist gave wonderful lectures on the evolution of rocks and birds. The rocks found on this planet were mostly some forms of granite and were pink and red. We saw many species of birds. The albatross is a big, graceful bird known for long-distance flights. The Cape petrels fly far from land and followed our boat. There are many types of gulls – numerous with long wings.

The ozone layer is decreasing significantly. The higher temperatures cause the melting of the icebergs. We spent a great deal of time discussing global warming. This scientist stressed the fact that there are now more people living on this planet than ever before. The carbon dioxide (**CO_2**) from people and chemicals, especially coal, is so detrimental to the ozone layer. He didn't think that countries such as China would ever stop using coal.

Antarctica has the greatest amount of solar radiation due to its position when the planet is at the closest elliptical orbit to the sun. The polar regions perhaps have some association with each other and have always exerted a great influence on the rest of the planet.

One day we visited a British station where three young people were studying the life of the penguin and the weather. There was also a museum of the studies done by several scientific stations that had been on the continent in the past. It was exciting there because it was the first time we actually set foot on the continent.

The Zodiac driver took us to the iceberg graveyard. The currents pushed the icebergs into cover where they became compacted and could not get released. To sit there and hear no sound at all was ethereal. We were surrounded by the color blue. This can only be seen by the naked eye. A camera cannot catch the beauty of it.

The ship's crew did all they could to make our trip fun. One night the bartender served drinks on 10,000-year-old ice from a glacier he had climbed. The chefs prepared an abundant barbeque on the deck of the ship. There we sat in our jackets in 35-degree weather, eating, while surrounded by icebergs.

Man's history of the continent is inspiring. More than 2,000 years ago, Greek writers described a large mass of land in the south of the world. Even though they had never seen it, they believed it must exist so that it could "balance" the load they knew about in the northern half of the world. They named this imagined land "Anta-Arkitas" meaning the opposite of the Arctic.

In 1578 Sir Francis Drake proved Antarctica was separated from any southern continent when he was blown into what became known as the Drake Passage – the confluence of the two greatest oceans on earth. The voyages of Vasco da Gama and Magellan were confirmed by the findings of Drake.

Roald Amundsen of Norway was the first person to stand at the South Pole in 1911. An Englishman, Captain Robert Falcon Scott, was unable to reach it. Amundsen won the race there. Captain Scott and his men died on his journey in 1912.

Eisenhower in 1959 said, "The continents should be open to all nations for scientific and peaceful activities." Forty-five nations signed this agreement.

The Montreal Protocol, a treaty signed in 1987 by many nations including the United States, agreed that no one will have permanent claim to the continent of Antarctica, and it be open to all scientific expeditions. The nations are working together to limit tourism and preserve everything about Antarctica and keep it as pristine as possible in the future. They are doing their best to put limitation on human activity. Humans must leave nothing and take nothing. I so much wanted to pick up a rock.

So, what is Antarctica? The windiest, driest, and coldest place on our planet and it's still the last untouched place in our world. It is also the brightest of all continents.

Antarctica is an enormous continent. Britain could fit into it more than fifty times. More than 99 percent is covered by ice. In places the ice is more than three miles thick. It is completely surrounded by the vast Southern Ocean, half of which freezes in winter. We all hope that it can be kept as God made it. What a transforming experience and adventure.

ANTARCTIC SURVIVOR, TOM CREAN

This is about a remarkable book about a remarkable man. We had planned a cruise of the Black Sea with some special friends. Then I needed to have an immediate back surgery. So next year would do. Then there was a war in Crimea in the Ukraine. Fletcher asked, "What other sign to do you want – not the cruise, the Black Sea."

We had travel insurance, but another time had to be planned within thirty days.

So, we decided to go to southern Ireland. We had been to a medical meeting and toured Northern Ireland. The land there was an environment that was quite spectacular really very close to Scotland.

This time we chose an auto venture through the southern part with Fletcher driving the car during the day. Each night we had a destination in a castle or hunting lodge. One night we found ourselves in a rustic hunting lodge near Kenmare on a bay of the Atlantic Ocean. The owner offered to take us to an ordinary Irish restaurant because the lodge didn't serve meals.

I looked at the picture on the wall of a man with a pipe holding puppies – the background was snow. In the restaurant I sat with my back toward the wall. Suddenly, it came back to me – Shackleton! When I said that name, a young man serving us hurriedly left the table. He came back with a middle-aged woman. I asked if that was Sir Ernest Henry Shackleton in a picture. She said not; it was Tom Crean, her grandfather. Tom Crean went on Antarctica adventures with Shackleton. They were interested that we had been to Antarctica. Of course, we bought the book, *Life of Tom Crean*. When we returned to the lodge, we had great difficulty deciding who was going to read it first because Fletcher speed reads. I must read every word and put a star by something I deem important. The book came to have a special meaning to us.

Tom Crean could have been a typical Irish farmer but came from obscurity to be one of the greatest characters in the history of Polar exploration. Even today people are still captivated by the tales of Scott and Shackleton – heroism, tragedy, bravery, fortitude, failures, and outstanding sagas of human achievements.

Crean sailed on three of the four expeditions. He was a colorful, polar, straightforward character. He showed extraordinary depths of courage and did some of the most incredible deeds in the most inhospitable, physically, and mentally demanding environment. There is a Mount Crean in Antarctica today.

The Southern Ocean had to be crossed. The ships were the *Endurance* and the *Discovery*. The ships sailed from New Zealand for the South Pole. Foul weather came, and they had to abandon ship. They built a hut and stayed there for months. They spent one hundred and seventy days floating as if on a lifeboat - and crossed 800 miles in the world's worst sea. Then they had to hike over ice, and then it was 490 days before they felt land. Many days were lost, and Shackleton missed the South Pole. Scott made a try, but failed and Crean found the remains of the polar party.

Crean was given accolades for the courage he showed on these voyages – sometimes singing and urging everybody not to quit. His leadership skills and ability to keep up morale helped others to survive the epic journey.

This book really sang to me -- what a great night in southern Ireland.

The *Endurance* was found recently – in good shape in the frigid waters. The decision was made not to move the ship in any way.

MACHU PICCHU, GALAPAGOS, ECUADOR
Machu Picchu

A friend had told us to sit on the left side of the train going up and the right side coming back. What marvelous advice! The rocky, churning river was fantastic. The ruins at the top were in the clouds, so we did not see as much as we hoped. The Incas built the city around 1450 but abandoned it a century later at the time of the Spanish Conquest. Machu Picchu was voted one of the new Seven Wonders of the World. There was a fashion show one night, and my eyes fell on a piece of orange jewelry made from a likeness of Inca art. It is now one of my prized possessions.

Galapagos.

We went to the islands on a small ship, taking two excursions out each day. We had a very informative young man as a guide. He gave special attention to me in my wheelchair. He saw that I went in the Zodiacs and helped me walk among the crabs and iguanas. We had read Darwin's book, so we knew exactly what we wanted to see. Fletcher was enthralled by the huge turtles. I found the flightless bird with only half a wing, very sad. The most beautiful of all was the Blue-footed Booby. This trip we found to be one of the most exciting, and informative of all.

Ecuador

Roses – that was the reason to see Ecuador. Fletcher wanted to see and study the rose plantations grown on the equator's perfect temperature and sunlight for roses. Two 747-type planes leave daily for Miami and Amsterdam filled with roses. The growing is all done by computer.

It happened to be Good Friday. We sat in the center of the city and watched a statue of the Virgin Mary being carried through the streets.

Leaving Ecuador, we arrived in Panama and had Sunday religious services. We were guests of a couple from St. Philip's in Charleston.

THAILAND

This was my trip, and we were there twice. The first time we went with a group from Clemson. Their main reason to go to Thailand was as a side trip, after attending a football game in Japan when Clemson played Duke. The next time we stopped there was on a trip to Nepal. I particularly wanted to stay in the beautiful Mandarin Oriental Hotel on Chao Phraya River.

When my granddaughter was married, she and her husband spent their honeymoon in Thailand – so Fletcher and I gave them a night in the Mandarin. Of course, it was spectacular for them – butler with Champagne tray, massage for two, etc. They loved it! The next morning, they left to spend the night in a tent on the beach for $7.00. As they left to go down the elevator, a passenger remarked, "I have never seen two people in this hotel with backpacks." In all our travels we spent time in just about anything, so one night in the Mandarin was quite a treat.

Thailand was just another southeast country called Siam. Today it has the second largest economy in Southeast Asia. One man may be said to be very much the reason for this – Jim Thompson. During World War II, he was stationed in this area. Thailand was an ally of Japan in that war. Jim Thompson stayed in Thailand after the war and helped develop the silk industry there. It became quite a success all over the world. Thai silk has much more body than Chinese silk. He has a lovely store that looks like one on Fifth Avenue. Many American decorators use this beautiful silk in vibrant colors.

One weekend Jim Thompson and friends spent some restful time in the mountains. After lunch many took a nap, but he went to walk along a jungle path. He was never heard of again- no trace of him – animal? Enemy? He might have been CIA during the war. There is a great biography of him that I have read many times.

Dinner in Nepal Jungle.

Martha feeding elephant.

Enjoying jungle library.

Hunting tigers on elephant.

Getting on Zodiak to see penguins. Standing on Antarctica.

Fletcher and giant tortoise in Galapagos.

Taken from Nepali building –
Swastika.

Panama and Cuna Indians.

Taj Mahal

Searching for animals in Tanzania.

Accommodations in Tanzania.

Visiting Masai tribe.

Picture on wall of Tom Crean.

Pride of Lions – Fletcher painted this.

Hitler's home in Berchtesgaden.

Holocaust monument in Berlin.

GENOA

Fletcher was a trustee at Clemson University for nearly thirty years. He wanted to be familiar with all that the university offered to its students. So, we decided to pay a visit to Clemson's architectural center in Genoa, Italy, known as the Charles E. Daniel Center for Building Research and Urban Studies. Operated by the Clemson Architectural Foundation, the school is nicknamed "The Villa" because it is held in an historic nineteenth century villa.

We ate with the students and attended some of their classes. A Clemson professor is there for all the semesters. In addition, there are three Genovese professors. The students usually attend their junior year (usually just one semester). There is a summer minor program also. Genoa is a perfect site for such a program. Rail transportation is easily available and affordable to travel all over Europe. There is such an abundance of art and architecture to be enjoyed and studied. In addition, Genoa is noted for its many examples of Medieval, Renaissance, Baroque, and Gothic architecture. The University of Genoa (founded 1471) is an important center of higher learning in northern Italy.

The student's regular tuition pays the basic costs. The Clemson Architectural Foundation helps with all the other expenses. There are other groups that study landscape and building function. The center, organized by its mentor, Dean Harlan McClure, celebrated its 50th anniversary in 2022.

CEO and founder of Trident Construction, Robbie Fairey, spent some of his time at Clemson at Genoa studying construction. He has been very successful primarily in the Charleston area. He calls his time in Genoa incredible in so many ways. One of the most memorable times in his life he said, "spending five months living in Italy at the Villa gave me so many unforgettable memories as well as the unique opportunity to travel throughout Europe and experience many different cultures – not to mention the incredible architecture we were able to visit."

Professor John Jacques, who lives in Oregon, was so helpful in telling me of his thirty years as a professor of architecture and teaching in Genoa.

We were impressed and happy that Clemson students have such wonderful opportunities.

ARBEIT MACHT FREI "WORK MAKES YOU FREE" (POLAND)

Poland has always fascinated me. It truly was the battleground of Europe. When either Germany or Russia was at war, their battles went right across Poland. What brave people in an unfortunate piece of land.

We traveled by rail and decided to stop at Auschwitz. We had been to Dachau – but wanted to compare the two. I was in my wheelchair, and we traveled past all the containers of shoes, spectacles, hair, and that was so sad. Then we entered an area with a small café. It was cold and rainy, and I asked Fletcher to get me a cup of tea. He handed it to me, and my hands were shaking so I could not hold the container. I simply couldn't go on – so Fletcher went – and when he told me about it later, I was glad I didn't continue. More than 1.1 million people died at Auschwitz including nearly 1 million Jews. Those who were not sent to the gas chambers were sentenced to forced labor. How could such cruelty and suffering be!

It seems our American planes couldn't liberate the camp because to knock out the machine guns, the planes had to fly at a low altitude, and they were in real danger. Auschwitz closed in January 1945 with its liberation by the Soviet Army. Forced death marches killed nearly 60,000 prisoners when the Germans knew the Russians were coming.

So, we started on the pleasant side of our trip – and what a pleasure it was. It was Sunday afternoon in Warsaw and a large garden where many people were enjoying a Chopin concert. He is one of my favorite composers, and Fletcher had a hard time getting me to leave. After all that sorrow, we were - just hours away - enjoying such beauty.

The next morning, we called a cab. Fletcher said, "My wife collects pottery, so take us to buy some Polish pottery." The driver turned around and looked at Fletcher and said, "Better than alcohol or drugs!" I bought some nice Christmas presents.

The Island of Nevis
Alexander Hamilton by Ron Chernow

This book by Ron Chernow is a superb study of a man so important in American history. To write about this book is very difficult, but also a pleasure. Why am I so interested? There is the Broadway musical about him with all kinds of awards today. We attended a conference in Nevis, a small island in the West Indies, and visited Hamilton's birthplace and home from his early life.

Family: His mother was Rachel Faucette, probably of French Huguenot ancestry. James Hamilton was his father. James was a fourth son of a Scottish lord. There is no record of a marriage. This did not keep Hamilton from showing his brilliance. He said, "My birth is subject to the most humiliating creation." Rachel married again, which was unfortunate. The wedding took place at The Grange, her sister's plantation on St. Croix. Hamilton named the house he built in New York, The Grange. In an unfortunate set of circumstances, Rachel was accused of adultery. Chernow speculates much unhappiness for her.

Hamilton was a distinctly Scottish man in appearance – red hair and blue eyes. He and his mother spoke French much better than other founding fathers. His mother's influence made him conspicuous among the founding fathers as an advocate for freedom and abolition. His mother disappeared, but he did have some contact with his father through life.

Two men in the import-export business hired him. This is the first time his brilliance was noticed. He had always been a ferocious reader. He wrote an account of a hurricane; and his employers sent him to Boston and New York to study. His talent was the use of words – this followed him through life.

Association with Washington: He was made aide-de-camp to Washington who acted as a father for him. He was doing well in life with this influence. He had studied law, and this helped him in politics, at which he did exceedingly well.

Eliza Schuyler: His marriage opened many doors for him. He was now in the aristocratic world. She was to provide much support for him all his life. His father-in-law was a member of Continental Congress. This marriage was now a necessary part of his life, giving him political support from a blue-ribbon family.

The Reynolds affair: Hamilton became involved with Maria Reynolds, a beautiful married woman. It was well known as Maria's husband blackmailed him, seeking cash and political appointment. The affair and its consequences were a longtime embarrassment.

Religion: Hamilton's religion, as a youth, was an orthodox and conventional Presbyterianism. As an adult, he became influenced by Deism. However, he never doubted Christianity as the basis of law and morality. He had respect for other religions – Judaism, Catholicism, Islam – and supported religious freedom.

Political affairs: Hamilton helped shape our country: his position as a close advisor to George Washington, his co-authorship of the Federalist Papers, his role in the adoption of the United States Constitution, his establishment of the U.S. Mint and the Bank of the United States, his influence on foreign policy, his encouragement of industrial growth, etc. Hamilton wanted a strong central government. Theodore Roosevelt praised his leadership on a strong central government. It was as Secretary of the Treasury that Hamilton had the most influence, establishing a strong financial base for the country.

Hamilton's nationalism put him at odds with Thomas Jefferson, who favored an agrarian economy and state's rights. However, Jefferson's Treasurer, Albert Gallatin, said Hamilton's economic program for the country was the most marvelous plan, and he could not do better.

I went to New York in 2004 for the opening of the exhibit, "Alexander Hamilton: The Man who Made Modern America." The New York Historical Society building had bunting all over the outside.

He and Aaron Burr were political enemies. Although they were neighbors on what is now Wall Street, Hamilton allegedly made a defamatory remark about Burr which became public. Burr and Hamilton could not reconcile – a duel became necessary. Hamilton's shot broke a limb over Burr's head. Burr shot Hamilton in the abdomen – a fatal wound. He died the next day. There was controversy as to who fired the first shot according to Hamilton's biographer, Ronald Chernow.

Chernow wrote his biography to better understand Hamilton's background, power, and contributions to our country. Chernow's *Alexander Hamilton* is one of the favorite books in my library.

He was truly a founding father of our country. Certainly, the visit to his birthplace in Nevis made quite an impression.

BARBADOS

The Charleston Museum planned a tour for Charlestonians who wished to visit the island to sightsee and search for early ancestors.

Englishmen were planting sugar there as early as the 1630s. Sugar production led to the expansion of slavery, and a huge slave trade linked Barbados with West Africa. Later, Barbadians helped establish Carolina and brought with them the plantation system, slavery, and the slave trade. In the eighteenth century, several prominent Charlestonians headed a triangular trade linking Charleston, England, and West Africa. In Great Britain, William Wilberforce led the movement for Parliament to end the slave trade in 1807, and slavery in the British Empire in 1833. Mandated by the U.S. Constitution, Congress ended the foreign slave trade in 1808. The lucrative days of slave trading in the Atlantic were over.

Many of the Barbadians wanted more land and Carolina had that; in 1670 the ship *Carolina* sailed into Charleston Harbor with immigrants from Barbados, England, and Ireland. Sir John Colleton, a Barbadian planter and merchant, was one of the eight Lords Proprietors of Carolina, with a huge land grant from Charles II. The Carolina grant began on the Atlantic coasts of present-day South Carolina, North Carolina, and Georgia and extended westward to the Pacific Ocean.

During the first decade of settlement, 1670-1680, about 50 per cent of the settlers arrived on ships from Barbados. Barbados was the wealthiest British colony in the seventeenth century. Charleston became the wealthiest city in America in the eighteenth century with an economy centered on the plantation system, slavery, and maritime commerce, all based on Barbadian models.

Our trip was delightful, with a lunch every day like what we would have in Charleston in the summertime – beef stew, rice and peas. The water was wonderful for swimming and the beach for watching the sun go down.

Charleston and Barbados have a long history of working together. We have had friendly diplomatic relations with the Barbados government and its people since our consular service was created by Congress in 1792.

PANAMA

An exciting part of the trip – other than riding along the canal – was flying over the Panamanian jungle in a single engine plane to visit the Cuna Indians (sometimes referred to as Guna Indians). This indigenous group of people live on small islands off the coast of Panama in the Caribbean known as the San Blas Islands. There are groups of Cuna that now live in Panama City, Colon, and other cities.

We landed on a very small "piece of land." It was the smallest I have ever seen, and I really thought we were going to land in the ocean.

An American who lived on a boat was our guide. The Cuna people were like none we had ever seen. They are very small – not quite 5 feet tall – very dark skinned, straight black hair and extremely high cheek boned. They are very like natives of South America, except in the height. The population is around 50,000 people. They speak a Cuna language and have traditional religious beliefs.

We found them very friendly, particularly when we bought some of their molas. Their molas consist of different color cloth depicting scenes of animals and events in their lives. Mola vendors can be found in most cities in Panama. I bought four of the molas, but they were destroyed in storage.

The Cuna have a long, deep-rooted history of mercantilism. They import goods from Columbia, Mexico and China ships and sell them in small retail stores that they own. This tradition of trade and self-determination has been credited by many as the chief reason the Guna have been able to successfully function independently compared to other indigenous groups. Guna communities in Panama City are usually made up of migrant laborers and small business owners. Tourism is now an important part of their economy.

Guna families are matrilineal and matrilocal with the groom moving to become part of the bride's family. The groom also takes the last name of the bride. The Gunas' health is notable; they have a low average blood pressure, and cardiovascular disease and cancer are rare.

They do have a high incidence of albinism. These led to the nickname "white Indian" in the early 1900s. In Guna tradition albinos are given a special place and are considered a special race of people. According to Wikipedia. org: "They have the specific duty of defending the Moon against a dragon which tries to eat it on occasion during a Lunar eclipse, and only they are allowed to go outside on the night of a Lunar eclipse and to use specially made bows and arrows to shoot down the dragon." The albinos were especially interesting to me as I saw some now and then when I was growing up in Orangeburg. They constitute about 0.7 percent of the Guna population and are not permitted to intermarry.

Religious centers called Shamas care for the sick and practice various types of witchcraft. We saw the practices of Shamas in Costa Rica. The sun and moon were formerly major deities, but the mythology has been much affected by European connections.

Our white Christian guide was very vocal about missionaries who come, and that persuaded some Guna to accept Christianity. He thought that it helped them in the cities, to get better jobs to better themselves, but that it often leads to alcoholism.

According to Wikipedia.org: "The Guna flag was adopted after the 1925 rebellion against Panamanian suppression. Horizontal stripes have a proportion of 1:2:1 and the central swastika is an ancestral symbol called Naa Ukuryaa. According to one explanation, it symbolizes the four sides of the world or the origin from which peoples of the world emerged. In another explanation, it symbolizes the octopus that created the world, its tentacles pointing to the four cardinal points. Also known as the flag of Guna Yala Island today, the flag was used for the province of San Blas until 2010 and is used as the Guna ethnic flag. The central stripe, meaning peace and purity, is white on the official flag of the reservation, officially adopted by Guna National Congress, while yellow stripe is used on the ethnic flag (it was introduced on the flag at about 1940). In 1942 the flag was modified with a red ring (representing the traditional Guna nose-ring) encompassing the center of the swastika. Because of Nazi associations, the ring was later abandoned."

CAMBODIA

It was Fletcher's idea to go to Cambodia, determined to see Angkor Wat. There were many other places I would rather have gone.

Cambodia is in the southern portion of Indochina in Southeast Asia. It has a population of over seventeen million people. The ancient Kingdom of Cambodia became part of French Indochina, was occupied by the Japanese, ruled by the Khmer Rouge, who murdered many of the inhabitants, and dominated by Communist North Vietnam. Under United Nations sponsorship, it became free again in 1993. It is a constitutional monarchy with a prime minister and parliament.

Buddhism is enshrined in the constitution as the official religion. There are religious structures throughout the country. Angkor Wat is the most famous of these; dating from the twelfth century, it is the largest temple in the world, and is designated as a World Heritage Site.

We arrived early one morning with our guide. I was scared because it was right at dawn, and we were the only people there. Our guide said the others' buses would come soon!

Two young girls appeared and handed me a piece of cloth. I asked, "What should I do with this?" "Place it on your table, Madame," one of the girls said. Fletcher said, "Buy it, Martha, if she can speak such perfect English where we are."

Fletcher was entranced with the structure – walked all around it and over it. Years later, I am convinced he was on CIA business that day. I was just glad to leave – too spooky.

INDIA

Many people tried to talk us out of going to India – everybody says they get sick in India. We ate toast and coffee for breakfast. I bought a box of nabs for lunch with a Coke. For dinner we ate in a very nice hotel. We had been told not to drink the bottled water. Fletcher had plenty of pills to cure that – and some to take the smell away. We did it and we didn't get sick.

The first sight of the Taj Mahal is fantastic. It almost literally "takes your breath away," it is so beautiful. I wanted to study each little part of the marble structure and how it is put together; it was something I had never seen anywhere before. Of course, we had our picture taken on the bench.

There happened to be a wedding in our hotel. The wedding party all wore pastel shades of silk. It was an outstanding picture of loveliness.

After touring the triangle around New Delhi, we left India, wanting to return.

SCOTLAND

We went on an auto trip through Scotland. We were given an itinerary which we didn't always follow. We only visited one Scotch whiskey showroom where there had been about eight suggested. I located Glamis Castle, the childhood home of the late Queen Mother and the birthplace of Princess Margaret. It is a stark castle with round towers and a fascinating interior. It is located near Balmoral – very easy for Elizabeth Bowes-Lion to date her future husband, George VI.

Culloden House and Moor, just east of Inverness, is a mansion built about 1780. When we arrived, the sunlight was beautiful on the Virginia Creeper vine covering almost all the house. Almost all the field of the great battle of Culloden is moorland. We were able to walk around and study the directions of the battle. In 1745 the young Pretender, "Bonnie Prince Charlie" landed in Scotland with a handful of men, raised an army and invaded England. His forces suffered a devastating defeat at Culloden Moor. The prince became a fugitive and was captured on the Isle of Skye. That was the end of his attempt to become the Catholic King of England.

After a night in the luxurious Culloden Manor, we took the bridge road to Skye; it was beautiful, though the bridge was scary. We ended our tour of Scotland at a bed and breakfast owned by a lady who had a cooking school. We had one of the most delicious meals.

SCANDINAVIA

We gave the children their choice of a country – so we toured all of Scandinavia especially Oslo and Stockholm. Of course, we saw the little mermaid at Copenhagen. We had a delightful few days with Dr. Bruno Dahlberg in Sweden. He lived in Malmo, and we took the exciting hovercraft trip from Copenhagen. He and Fletcher had become very good friends, being on some of the same medical programs. He came to see us often in the States. Bruno was a gracious host and gave me my first piece of amber.

We also saw Dragsholm Castle near Copenhagen in Denmark, where Mary Queen of Scots' husband was imprisoned. James Hepburn, Earl of Bothwell, was accused of murdering Mary's previous husband, Lord Darnley. The Scots revolted and defeated Bothwell at the Battle of Carberry Hill. He fled to Norway, where he was arrested by the Danish King Frederick II and taken to Dragsholm where he died ten years later.

MONT SAINT MICHEL

Our family had a fantastic trip to Normandy when our children were six and twelve years old. We all were very quiet when we walked through the graves in the American cemetery – so many. Carl and I gathered shells on the beach, and I just could imagine the heroism there that day.

Then we took a journey that was so like a fairytale it is hard to describe. We spent the day at Mont Saint Michel when the tide was out and made it a point to return before the tide changed. If you spend the night, there is special parking. This was so interesting to me because when I was a young girl, I saw a movie about this starring Lana Turner and Van Heflin. Another actress was caught by the tide and had to climb up through the center – very exciting!

The climb up all those steps to the church at the top was not as difficult as it was exciting to see all sorts of people climbing with us. We stayed a while at the church and then made ourselves come down. The religious experience in the church is something none of us will forget. Carl, who was six years old, remarked this was where he wanted to spend his honeymoon. Coming down we stopped at a restaurant and had the most delicious waffles. My whole family believes this was one of our most favorite and exciting trips to be remembered.

A WEEKEND IN NOVA SCOTIA

Some friends invited us to Nova Scotia for a special birthday party. Dr. Dabney Jarman was going to be ninety. He was the chairman of the committee that brought Fletcher to George Washington University as Chairman of Urology. He was always so nice to us, and saw that Fletcher was welcomed and included as part of the Washington urological world.

There was one object in the way – I was in horrible pain and needed back surgery. But Fletcher wanted to go.

The party was a great success, and Dr. Jarman was so delighted and surprised to see Fletcher.

Standing up at the party was really difficult for me. The only thing that helped was that Dr. Jarman's son-in-law, Mr. Gantner, was an editor for *National Geographic*. I really enjoyed talking to him.

When the party was over and we were in the car going back to our hostess' home, she announced, "We have invited some of our friends to our house tomorrow night to meet you." My heart fell; I just didn't think I could attend a party for hours. Fletcher said I had to; we were the guests of honor.

I took two pain pills and Fletcher prepared me some kind of drink. I did it! Fletcher said the next morning I didn't embarrass myself and that I was quite charming. I don't remember anything about it. It is all a blank.

We left the next day, and I went straight to the hospital for back surgery.

PORTUGAL AND SPAIN

We had wonderful days driving around the countryside, staying in castles or bed and breakfasts. We loved all the cork trees, and I bought a bowl made of cork.

Driving through Portugal, suddenly, we found ourselves in a traffic jam. It looked like the Carolina/Clemson game – everybody was tailgating and having a wonderful time. Of course, we investigated, and it turned out we were in Fatima where young children had seen The Virgin in 1917. It has become a place of pilgrimage.

People were crawling on their knees to get to the shrine in hopes of being healed. We just watched and found ourselves praying with these brave people. This was something we found very inspiring and a plus to our trip. Their hope was beautiful.

In Spain we enjoyed the Prado in Madrid, and spending the night in a house in Trujillo, used by students at Coker College and the College of Charleston. The College of Charleston has an annual spring semester program in Trujillo, where classes are held in the Coria, a seventeenth century convent.

MASADA, AD 73

HEROD. The same King Herod who the Three Wise Men came to see, seeking Jesus. The Gospel of Matthew tells us that he slaughtered all the young infants in Bethlehem, out of fear that a Messiah would replace him as king of the Jews. He was half Jewish; his father was Jewish and his mother Arab. He was determined to keep peace in Israel and remain absolute in his power as a Roman puppet king. He ruled Judea for many years. Throughout his life, he blended creativity, cruelty, harmony, and chaos. Josephus, the first century historian, described his horrible, painful death: burning fever, ulcerated entrails, foul discharges, stench, etc. Josephus wrote that it was a judgment from God for Herod's many sins. The American Urological Association has determined he died of a rare gangrene of the genitalia, as well as chronic kidney disease. He was a ruthless tyrant.

FLAVIUS SILVA. A general of Rome's undefeated 10th legion.

ELEAZER. The fiery leader of the Jewish rebels – rag dog band of rebels, hot tempered renegade soldiers – life or death mentality. All we know about Masada is written by Josephus – a person who made sure he was on the right side with the Romans. It is described as the most desolate part of the wilderness – maybe the most desolate wilderness on earth – and it may be the same wilderness Jesus retreated to after baptism. Masada is situated on an isolated rock on the edge of the Judean desert and the Dead Sea Valley (approximately 1,300 feet to the shore of the Dead Sea). Its western side is approximately 330 feet high above sea level. The rock is shaped very narrow in the north and broad in the center and is 1,950 feet from north to south and approximately 1,000 feet from east to west in the center. Its natural approaches are steps and paths. It creates airy and luminous residues that were also a virtually impregnable fortress. The day I was there, it was 125 degrees – I could not place my hand on the railing as I walked the stairs. There are 300 steps to the top. All my eighteen-year-old son remembers of the day is heat and dust. He walked up the mountain – following a path already there. We were all at the top taking a tour and someone yelled, "Here comes Carl."

On this spot a new Herod is seen – an exceptional architect using remarkable scope, ambition, and creativity to build a magnificent palace here – a virtual paradise with many baths and all amenities known at the time. It is a black and white mosaic floor in geometric designs and is one of the earliest mosaics found in Israel. Containing scores of rooms and installations, these palaces were self-sufficient and consisted of four wings – a large splashing swimming pool overlooked the scenery and terraced gardens. There was a furnace to provide hot water when Herod was here. There was food for 10,000 soldiers stored there. Herod constructed cisterns which held 10,000 gallons of water. This was indeed a self-sufficient citadel.

There had been many revolts by the Jews against Rome. This was probably the last and most well-planned. The Jewish rebels retreated to Masada. Silva's effort to conquer Masada is still clearly visible. He surrounded the fortress with wall fortified by towers to prevent the 960 defenders from escaping. Around the base of Masada, he set up eight camps, including one that served as his headquarters. After many months and all else failed, he was able to build an assault ramp of beaten earth and large stones on which was erected a siege tower from which the wall was attacked with a battering ram, catapults, and flaming torches.

Eleazer and his followers were determined not to be taken alive and be Roman prisoners or slaves. Their action at this time has been disputed by some modern archaeologists, but which Josephus described, after interviewing some eyewitnesses.

The casting of lots was a known practice among the Jews. The disciples of Jesus cast lots to replace Judas with Mathias. Something like this was used at the foot of the cross for the garment of Jesus.

Eleazer and his men drew lots; then many were killed by slitting the throats. Each man killed his family, lots were cast again and again until only one man remained. This one man was the only one to commit suicide. Suicide is forbidden in Jewish culture. They believe, as we Christians do, that only God takes away life; it is not ours to give. To do so today, means you cannot be buried in a Jewish cemetery unless under unusual circumstances. There is one alternative – you are going to be killed anyway – suicide was the only way. But only God, not Romans, determined this.

When the Roman troops entered Masada, they were met by an eerie silence – no one alive, but a few women who told what happened. The Romans were denied a victory.

Masada became a symbol of the founding of Israel in 1948. They vowed they would never be slaughtered again. The cry was like the Alamo – "Remember Masada." The Jews used this patriotic cry for many years and soldiers were inducted into the Israeli army on top of Masada. This is not done today, and the rhetoric has been toned down. Israel did not want to appear too radical. The question was to die for one's dream or to dream for another day.

So today it is a tourist attraction if you can stand the heat. And we can find Israel again fighting what they see as a holy war for their very existence.

All of us want peace. We must pray for peace in the Middle East. Do we have a fight for it? Yes – Isaiah 26 says, "Thou shall keep him in perfect peace, whose mind is stayed on this." Relying on God is the ultimate fight in life. Give me, O God, this day a strong vivid sense that thou art by my side.

Swimming in the Dead Sea

Carl and I could hardly wait to get in the water. We bounced up and down, unable to swim – what fun! The Dead Sea is the lowest point on this earth. After we had our fun, we took a public shower. My ring had never had such sparkle.

FOLLOWING THE JOURNEYS OF PAUL

I have long had something like a love affair with the Apostle Paul since I took a course in his journeys while in college. So, when the opportunity came to take a cruise following his second and third missionary journeys, with a side trip to the Isle of Patmos, I knew I had to go. I had to see for myself the travail he endured as he encouraged Christianity in Asia Minor and spread it to the European world.

Paul was preaching Jesus as the promised Messiah. He was not preparing a holy war to conquer as Caesar, as some who heard him wished; he simply came to Jerusalem unarmed on the back of a donkey on what Christians came to call Palm Sunday. He came to conquer men's souls, not earthly kingdoms. Nothing stopped Paul, not shipwreck, rivers, mountains, deserts, threats, hunger, lashing, stoning, being beaten with rods, or imprisonment.

Paul's Earlier Life

The Apostle Paul was indeed the perfect man for this undertaking. He was a Jew born in Tarsus (Asia Minor) in what is today Turkey. He was the son of a Pharisee of the tribe of Benjamin. How Paul became a Roman citizen is not known, but such citizenship saved his life many times because Roman citizens could not be crucified. His citizenship also enabled him to preach the gospel and carry out his mission to the Gentiles.

He was a tentmaker, a trade that would have benefited the Roman generals. Paul took great pride in being from Tarsus and may have belonged to the city's upper social ranks. Tarsus was a great commercial city, and Paul was exposed to its language, literature, and philosophy. His training under Gamaliel was the finest. He hated the Christian faith and was traveling to Damascus to capture Christians. There he personally met Jesus Christ. After this confrontation he was never the same.

Neither Paul nor anyone else claimed that Paul met Jesus other than in his great epiphany. In fact, when the first Christian martyr Stephen was stoned to death, Paul held the coats of the participants. Then, when he was on the way to persecute Christians on the road to Damascus, Jesus appeared to him in a great light.

Journeys to Macedonia and Greece

Paul had a vision directing him to Macedonia. The vision said, "Come over to Greece," and the fruit of his obeying the vision was his first convert to Christianity at Philippi, a certain Lydia, a "seller of purple goods." Philippi had a special meaning to Fletcher and his sister Betty, who was on the trip with us. Their family had once belonged to the Philippi Baptist Church which was near their home. Here also Paul was jailed and converted the jailer and his household. During our visit to Philippi, we sat by the small river where Lydia was probably baptized and sang "Amazing Grace."

It was a special occasion to stand on Mars Hill under the Acropolis where Paul stood and preached. Paul saw in Athens an altar with the inscription, "To an unknown God," and there he delivered his famous sermon about that God. Although Athens was the artistic, philosophic, and religious capital of the world, Paul still had some converts there.

Corinth, uniformly pagan, was known as the most beautiful city in Greece. Two of Paul's letters that he wrote back to this city discuss the many issues the Jewish converts had to deal with now that they were Christians and still surrounded by Jewish tradition and living in a Roman culture. The well-known chapter on love, beginning, "If I speak in the tongues of men and of angels," was written to this congregation of Christians in ancient Corinth.

Thessalonica was the center of Paul's missionary activities in northern Greece. The city had a multicultural ethnic society and may have had difficulty accepting Paul's message that we are all "One in Christ." His first converts there were a "great many of the devout Greeks and not a few of the leading women." As always, there was persecution. Paul encouraged the congregation to endure that. Despite hardships, the Thessalonians became an example to all believers.

Paul's Journey to Asia Minor

Seeing the excavations that have been done in Ephesus was a memorable experience. It was the most important seaport in Asia Minor and one of the largest cities in the Roman Empire. Paul's friends, Priscilla and Aquila, worked with him there. Paul was to make this city the center from which he evangelized the whole province of Asia Minor. The streets of Ephesus were lined with temples, whose remains are now evident, and many pagan cultures worshipped in the city. The temple of Artemis was one of the Seven Wonders of the Ancient World. Paul spoke there of a world which binds together all people into one family of God. This was a new concept of the future of the church under the leadership of Christ.

The great amphitheater at Ephesus seats 24,000 people, and our group had a very emotional communion service there. Several people read from Paul's letters to the Ephesians from different places in the amphitheater.

Pergamum, north of Ephesus, was an important and wealthy city in the Roman Empire because of its famous healing center which the Roman Emperors visited. The Asclepieion was known as the final medical healing center for those who had not been helped by their local physicians. The healing was after the style of Asclepius, Apollo's son, the god of medicine. Many temples or shrines were connected to the healing center. Harmless Asclepian snakes were used in the healing centers. Paul had many converts there, but they were persecuted, and the first Christians were killed by the Romans there. Paul exhorted the church there to hold fast to the faith and to deny false doctrines in their midst.

Patmos

Our last stop on the tour was the Isle of Patmos where the apostle John wrote the book of Revelation. He had been exiled in a cave there. There is now a church standing above the cave.

This was one of our last trips because I wouldn't go on a Mediterranean cruise that didn't go to Patmos. I wanted to see the cave where John was exiled. Patmos is a small island – one shop where I bought a lovely plate. It was covered with dust. Evidently no one had seen the beauty in it until I came along. I went up all these steps to the Church and then the cave. The most beautiful cave I have ever seen, and it was enormous. John had a spectacular place to write all those wonderful letters. But it must have been lonely.

This is one place Fletcher and I had really wanted to return.

A VISIT TO MALTA
Published in the Charleston Mercury, July 30, 2009

Why Malta? Because of Paul, formerly Saul of Tarsus, but more on that in a moment. Malta is amazingly easy to reach by using almost all European airlines. In the heart of the Mediterranean, it is a melting pot of civilizations with a history stretching back thousands of years. The country has been inhabited since about 5,200 B.C.

The Phoenicians named the island Malta, meaning "safe haven." Its position in almost the center of the Mediterranean made it a chosen spot for ships and sailors. Many people have conquered it – Greeks, Romans, Carthaginians, Turks, Egyptians, and others. It would be interesting to have a DNA analysis of the people living there now. At some point Malta may have been a bridge of dry land to Africa, but long before prospering under the rule of Romans, who left many artifacts on the island which still exist.

In 60 A.D. Paul and Luke, Paul's amanuensis who was traveling with him, were shipwrecked on a beach in Malta. Luke, who wrote the Book of Acts, was a prisoner also headed for Rome for judgement. During the intense weeks-long storm, Paul told the passengers not to be afraid; all aboard the ship were saved. Paul said the people of Malta were kind to them, building a bonfire on the beach to welcome them and to warm them. Paul gathered some sticks for the fire and a poisonous snake fastened itself on his arm. He shook off the snake into the fire and was unharmed. The beach snake was thought to be a miracle, and as a result the Malta sand was thought to have a healing effect. Paul himself healed numerous people on the island. (See Acts 27 and 28). He spent several months healing people on the island – but he also spent months in prison with Luke.

Paul and Luke were still prisoners, though Paul would be free during the day because he was a Roman citizen. After 90 days, he had made Christians of the entire island. Our guide said that was true today except for a few Muslim and Jewish families.

A boat came by Malta every 30 days, so Luke and Paul went on to Rome. A lovely cathedral there built in his honor stands today above the grotto where he was imprisoned.

The Knights of the Order of St. John of Jerusalem, the full name of the Knights of Malta, were established in 1085 for a community of monks looking after the sick at the hospital of St. John. They later became a military order defending crusade territory in the Holy Land and safeguarding the perilous route for medieval pilgrims. Noble families of Europe had acquired vast wealth from recruiting and privateering, and they were supported with financial assistance from many different merchants in the Italian city of Amalfi. They came to Malta in 1530 and stayed 258 years. The order was ruled by a grand master who was answerable only to the pope. These knights were sworn to celibacy, poverty, and obedience. Some lived up to these ideals, but many were wealthy and tempted in various ways. The original Christian hospice may have been founded as early at 1020.

In modern times, Prince Phillip was stationed here in his early career with the Royal Navy. Princess Elizabeth spent some time on the island with him.

Our visit to Malta was all too short. It was the entrance of another small island into our lives. Malta's history is an integral part of western civilization. Malta today is a sun-drenched island of sandstone homes and buildings. All the trees are gone. It still has its wonderful harbor and Mediterranean personality. St. Paul may have felt he had a new life after surviving that horrible shipwreck and landing on such a friendly island.

ROME

Paul writes in Second Corinthians that he had a "Thorn in his flesh" by the messenger Satan. He "besought the Lord thrice" that it might go away because what he believed was a hindrance to his work. History never has determined if the "thorn" was malaria, epilepsy, or a disease of the eyes (Jesus appeared to him in a bright light when he was on the road to Damascus and he was blinded for three days). Also he was a tentmaker in Tarsus and his fingers may have been gnarled. Any of these reasons may have required an amanuensis (secretary) and Luke was perfect for that job. Luke was a physician and could treat physical ailments as well as knowing Jesus.

The thorn kept Paul humble. It reminded him of his need for constant contact with God, and benefited those around him as they saw God at work in his life.

The legend is that Paul was beheaded just outside the walls of the City of Rome where a church stands today. Fletcher and I found the church and the spot where he supposedly died. Christians believe that nothing happens by chance alone, that God used Paul for the important task of spreading the gospel to the known world. We came away from the trip believing that God did prepare Paul with all the attributes that made him the perfect one for the undertaking. He was indeed a man who never lost his passion for spreading Christianity.

Paul hinted of a fourth missionary journey. Tradition says he went to Spain. When Fletcher and I were in Spain, we toured an old Jewish village in eastern Spain. I could imagine Paul walking the same streets. Some people have said that I am too attached to Paul. All I know is that he took the Gospel of Jesus to the western world. After Jesus ascended into heaven, he told disciples to go all over the world preaching the good news. Tradition tells that most of the disciples went East and South. Paul had that wonderful education from Gamalial, and he was a Roman citizen so he went to Greece, Rome, etc. It then was carried by colonization to you and me. How fortunate we are that he came West.

Israel

I went to Israel twice. The first time, Fletcher and I attended a medical meeting in Tel Aviv. The first Roman Emperor to convert to Christianity was Constantine in c. 330 AD. His mother - Helena - took a journey to the Holy Land to discover the places associated with the life of Jesus. The guide we had took us to those places. The second trip, we were very fortunate (my 17-year-old son Carl and I) to go with our minister we had in Washington. Tom Jackson had a Ph.D. from Johns Hopkins in Near Eastern history, and his knowledge certainly made our trip more interesting. He took us to a differnt site for the cross and the tomb – outside of the city – which has been identified by an Englishman named Gordon in the twentieth century. The Romans usually executed their crucifixtions on the highways leading into the city to advertise punishments for crimes.

What a joy it was to walk where Jesus walked.

Russia

St. Petersburg was fantastic. We had a young girl as a guide. She could have not been nicer. She suggested we start early at the Hermitage to have plenty of time to study the impressionist paintings. We did go there first and after several hours Fletcher didn't want to leave. We had it all to ourselves.

Our luck in Moscow wasn't the same. We had the worst guide we ever had in all our travels. He wouldn't take us to see what we wanted to see.

To start – the first place he took us was an old building containing two big bombs which he said, "one was intended for New York and one for Washington." I don't know what reaction he wanted from us, but we had none; we just stood there.

We very much wanted to study Red Square and the people entombed there. He rushed us through so we could count the diamonds on the Czarina's wedding gown.

The ballet was closed when we were there, so we went to the symphony. Rachmaninoff was wonderful. We had the last two seats at the very top of the beautiful concert hall but heard every note. It was magnificent.

Getting back to the hotel was somewhat of a problem. It was still daylight, but no taxis. The mass of people all came on buses. Fletcher called the hotel; immediately a huge black car came with a very frustrated driver. He was very upset about where we were, but the hotel had sold us the tickets!

Our Russian visit ended joyfully when some students from Syracuse carried my wheelchair up and down three steep flights of stairs. They were so helpful at the concert. The Syracuse dean came to Clemson for a ballgame, and Fletcher told him all about that delightful gesture.

ESTONIA

I was packing to leave Russia and catch the plane back to the States, when Fletcher told me we had one more stop before going home – Estonia. I knew very little about Estonia and never dreamed of going there. Why there? I think I discovered the reason we went.

It was a lovely little village just along the water. We joined a group and walked along the very pristine attractive streets. I was thoroughly enjoying it. Then we stopped for lunch at a wonderful restaurant. Suddenly Fletcher whispered in my ear, "I'll be right back." Where was he going?

It would be about 30 years before I realized why he left me alone with all those people. **He had to meet someone for the CIA.** It all made sense when he told me about his clandestine life. So that was the reason we went to Estonia.

Bert & Jeanne Gue, Horry Kerrison & Robert Johnson.

Scottie & Robert Johnson in N.C. mountains.

Martha and Loraine Hanckel at wedding.

High School friends at San Francisco wedding Pat Duncan and Emma Montgomery.

Betty (sister) and Fletcher's mom with Ginny and Tom Jackson – Minister at McLean, VA church.

High school friends – Melton Eargle, Henry Bair & Mary and Brown Bradley.

Frank Hanckel, Paul Wieters, Joe McDevitt.

Johnny Rodrigue & Martha at wedding.

McDevitts and Hanckels at Clemson.

Best friends in Medical school – `Si Ameen, Pat Dennis.

Carl's college roommate & best friend, Charlie Echols.

Dr. Dabney Jarman – Urologist, Washington.

Duplicate bridge partner, Mike – our highest game.

Martha consoles Dick Davenport after Hurricane Hugo destroyed his business.

FUNNIES

My Sansbury Grandmother said everything had to have a funny. So here goes.

Martha 1: My favorite piece of fiction when I was a young girl was *Les Misérables* by Victor Hugo. My children had not read it (this was before the musical). We were in Paris and had done several days of sightseeing. I proposed something different – a trip to the sewers of Paris to entice them to read the book. I wanted them to know of the beauty of the character Jean Valjean and his opposite in the life of Javert. We had a hard time getting directions to the sewers at the hotel. Finally, we found ourselves standing by the beautiful Seine River – and down some stairs. There we saw a slide movie of the sewers, and everybody seemed interested – I thought things were going well. Then there was a marvelous exhibit of the sewers that Fletcher found very fascinating. Then we walked along the actual sewers. Suddenly, Fletcher was not to be found. I hurried back up the stairs to find Fletcher hanging over the rail rather ill. He looked at me and said, "Do you have any more bright ideas?"

Martha 2: My high school Latin teacher talked a great deal of Julius Caesar, and how important it was when he crossed the Rubicon and gained control of the entire Roman Republic. Caesar is supposed to have said, "The die is cast." It came to mean, "The point of no return." Caesar then had a victory in a civil war and ruled Rome until his death. I have crossed many Rubicons in my life and wanted to see that famous river. We were in Italy several times and once in the central part near the Adriatic Sea. I asked Fletcher to please take me to see the Rubicon. That proved to be difficult. Finally, we asked directions – strange looks came our way. After many twists and turns, we came to it. It was a ditch about knee-high in water. Very dramatically Fletcher said, "Martha, here is your Rubicon – now what would you like to see next?"

Fletcher 1: Oh, how we loved our trip to Italy and particularly to Florence. The Uffizi Art Gallery was spectacular. I particularly was enchanted with Botticelli's Venus. We finally came to the end -- that unbelievable Michelangelo by David. Fletcher looked and said nothing then he blurted out, "He is a Jew and is not circumcised." I could not get him to hush. That is all he saw in this magnificent statue. There was a group of ladies from England standing next to us – horrified. I just looked at them and said very sadly, "He is a urologist." We then left and it was a long time before I took Fletcher to another art gallery. There is a movement in Florence to place a fig leaf over that certain part of his statue.

Fletcher 2: If you asked Fletcher his favorite trip, he would say immediately Egypt. Why? We stayed at that lovely Mena House right at the pyramids. Every morning we had coffee on our balcony overlooking those majestic structures. Was that what Fletcher liked? No. It was all the phallic symbols along the Nile and elsewhere. He just could not believe what he was seeing and took many pictures. One of his favorite lectures he loved to give was regarding phallic symbols in art and architecture. Oh, why couldn't I have married an ophthalmologist? I usually found an excuse not to go to the phallic lectures.

"DR. LIVINGSTONE, I PRESUME"

"Dr. Livingstone, I presume," is one of the most quoted sayings of the nineteenth century. It referred to a man who opened a new area in our world to the Gospel of Jesus Christ. As a young girl, I saw the movie about Livingstone, with Spencer Tracy playing Stanley. Never could I dream I would actually have the privilege to someday stand where Livingstone had stood.

Africa "called" to me and Fletcher. We went there five times. We knew about Dr. David Livingstone, missionary of the Gospel, medical doctor, explorer and earnest opponent of slavery, whose vision was to set many souls free of slavery – both spiritual and physical. Although he failed to locate the source of the Nile, his motive for searching for it was to gain a platform from which to denounce the slave trade. (This made him unpopular with the traders.) And everywhere he went, he told the story of Christianity.

Livingstone began traveling to Africa in 1841, and from then until his death in 1873, it is estimated that he traversed some 40,000 miles on the continent. On his first missionary journey, he went two years without seeing his family, having sent them home. He traveled hundreds of miles at a time and became very sick with malaria and other ailments. He explored the Zambezi River and was the first European to see Victoria Falls, and named it after his queen. He decided to travel north where the area was higher, fertile and free from malaria – a good place for a mission and trading station.

On his return trips to England, he was a celebrity for his exploits, and people were captivated by his story of a civilization on the African continent. Praise came from everywhere, and the Royal Geographic Society held a special meeting to welcome him. The Society awarded him their highest honor – their gold medal. They said, "You have accomplished more for the happiness of mankind than has been done by all the African traders put together."

He worked to convince his countrymen that Christianity and commerce were the keys to civilization. Dr. Livingstone did not like public speaking. In fact, he held his head down until he had to speak. He never lectured for a fee. He kept a busy schedule and did a voluminous amount of writing.

Livingstone, in 1866, returned to Africa and seemed to disappear. Nobody heard from him for nearly six years. Where was Dr. Livingstone?

Henry Morton Stanley was sent by the *New York Herald* to find Livingstone and spent two years looking for him. He went to many villages asking, "Do you know a white man?" Finally one man said "Jesus," and he knew Livingstone was near. He was told there was a white man at Ujiji, on the shore of Lake Tanganyika, and he found his quarry there on November 10, 1871. When he saw him, he raised his helmet and said, "Dr. Livingstone, I presume?"

Stanley was trembling with excitement to see Livingstone. Livingstone had tears in his eyes, and each lifted their cap to the other. Stanley brought generous supplies and the first letters Livingstone had received in years. Stanley did not count the cost of finding him; his was the scoop of the century.

Livingstone said to Stanley, "You have given me new life, and I began to recognize the hand of God overruling and kindly providing." Stanley wrote, "In him there is no guile."

Livingstone, through Stanley, made his cause against slavery known. Livingstone was known for his respectful treatment of Africans and said that anyone who lived among them felt they were his brothers. Fletcher and I found this to be true.

Stanley took some of Livingstone's journals, maps, and observations back to England. Stanley's arrival there created a storm. The British were embarrassed that a loudmouth American journalist had beaten them in the search for Livingstone. Stanley later went on his own expedition to the Congo.

A year and a half after the legendary meeting, Livingstone was dead.

On his four African expeditions, Livingstone experienced malaria, cholera, foot sores, exposure to leprosy, dysentery and tropical ulcers. He wrote, "I lost almost all of my teeth - and was stoned by suspicious tribes."

Every Sunday, Livingstone preached, despite pain and incredible hardships. Toward the end he became weary, repeatedly fainted, and finally was persuaded to be carried. On May 1, 1873, he was found dead kneeling by his bed - one of the world's most spiritual pioneers.

Livingstone's African converts took his body to Zanzibar for shipment to England. His heart and other organs were removed and buried. His body was preserved with salt and brandy. They walked more than 1000 miles with the body over difficult terrain; some died on the march. It took them months to reach the ship. Many of Livingstone's porters later worked in mission stations.

In London, there were skeptics. Was this really the body of Livingstone? There was a post-mortem report. Livingstone had been mauled by a lion once during his time in Africa. Sir William Fergusson had done his best to put his arm back in shape on one of his trips home. The physician found, in the skeleton, the same shoulder wound he had tried to repair. Here were tooth marks and bone splinters. Sir William said he had set his mind at rest – to identify the body of one of the greatest men of the human race.

Livingstone was the only pauper buried in Westminster Abbey with full state honors. He was an amazing explorer – his influence on slavery and ministry of souls was unequaled at that time. He influenced many missions after his death. His life was a testimony to the grace of God.

For Fletcher and me, to have watched the sunset on the Zambezi River and seen the rainbows at Victoria Falls, made us feel we had walked in the footsteps of one of the greatest men to have lived on earth.

SULLIVAN'S ISLAND

Through the years we vacationed around South and North Carolina, but our favorite place came to be Sullivan's Island. Fletcher found a small house on the front beach – Station 29 – he had great fun with it. It was sunk into a gun turret from World War II. So, it had a very good foundation. He tore down the small family room and left 3 bedrooms and 2 baths. Then he added a huge room with a vaulted ceiling and bedroom for us upstairs.

We wanted to share this house with groups having conferences, so I added 2 stoves and 2 refrigerators. Many people were able to enjoy it that way. But the important thing was how the Derricks enjoyed it. We each had a special memory. Mottie and Carl had house parties for their friends. Mottie and her family lived there for several months when they moved back to Charleston.

One of my high school friends from Atlanta stayed there with her husband May thru September (probably the ideal time with the beautiful yellow butterflies all around). Their presence brought more high school friends from as far as San Francisco. It was a party every night when poor Fletcher had to work. They were all there when hurricane Hugo hit. Fletcher and I were at a medical meeting in Germany. He had boards made for every window and numbered them. The group didn't know the number system. They said it was a riot trying to understand what Fletcher meant. They did well as only 4 windows blew out. The house stood because the contractor had banged the pilings (Fletcher paid the contractor extra for that).

Ours was the only house standing at the end of the island, however it had been hit by a huge wave and the floor buckled underneath. Carl and I went on a shrimp boat two days later and emptied the refrigerator. Carl found his beloved boat wrapped around a tree. It had been under the house and everything there was washed away.

Fletcher loved to fix things that were needed in the beach house. His favorite thing on the beach with the grandchildren was building sandcastles. He would do it for hours. He and Carl loved to go shrimping. Carl would throw the net and Fletcher would guide the boat in their favorite creek with the right tide. We would then have those sweet creek shrimp with grits for breakfast.

My favorite thing was walking on the beach. I walked four miles a day from Station 29 to the rocks at the lighthouse and back. Carl's lab, Garrison, always went with me.

Garrison was Carl's love. He would throw the ball in the air and Garrison would catch it. He also followed on the "skim board" on which Carl was a master.

We all had bikes and rode all over the islands – particularly to the center of the island for the New Year's Eve fireworks.

As we think of those years, they were some of our favorites and our family was brought closer together sharing many joys.

Front beach before hurricane.

Beach – after hurricane.

Gun turret under house.

Our boat found 5 blocks away.

Carl with Garrison.

Garrison's favorite thing with Jerry Giesy

Garrison playing.

Carl throwing shrimp net in favorite creek.

Spoleto musicians enjoying beach for a day.

My favorite beach picture – Fletcher with Heyward.

Fletcher, Martha, Jerry Giesy, urologist from Oregon.

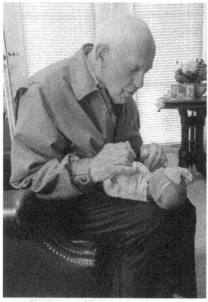

Last picture of Dr. Derrick, holding his first-born great grandchild, Louise Derrick McElwee.

Martha Derrick at the grave of Dr. Derrick six weeks after his death.

The author with great-granddaughter, Louise, in one of the gardens of Bishop Gadsden Retirement Community where she resides now.

"Let not your heart be troubled, neither let it be afraid."

Isaiah 43

But thus says the Lord
He who created you O Israel
I have called you by name
Thou art mine
When you pass thru the waters,
I will be with you.
And through the rivers,
They shall not overflow you
When you walk thru the fire
You will not be burned
And the flame will not consume you
For I am the Lord your God
Because you are precious in my sight
Thou hast been honorable
I have loved you – do not fear for I am with Thee.

BIBLIOGRAPHY

Alexander, Caroline. *The Endurance: Shackleton's Legendary Antarctic Expedition.* New York: Alfred A. Knopf, 1999.

Atkinson, Gene. "A History of Edisto Memorial Gardens." *The Times and Democrat*, March 1996.

Beccaceci, Marcelo. *Antarida/Antarctica: 100 Imagenes/100 Images* . No place: South World, 2007.

Bokenkotter, Thomas. *A Concise History of the Catholic Church.* New York: Doubleday and Co., 1979.

Bonhoeffer, Dietrich. *Life Together.* New York: Harper & Rowe Publishers, 1954.

Bradford, Ernle. *Gibraltar: The History of a Fortress.* New York: Open Road Media, 1971.

Caughman, J. Ansel. *A History of the Religious Life of Cedar Grove Community and Families Influencing its Culture.* Batesburg, S.C.: Bruner Press, 1952.

Chernow, Ron. *Alexander Hamilton.* New York: Penguin Press, 2004.

[Clayton, Matt.] *The Phoenicians: A Captivating Guide to the History of Phoenicia and the Impact Made by One of the Greatest Trading Civilizations of the Ancient World.* No place: Captivating History, 2019.

Conze, Edward. *Buddhism: Its Essence and Development.* New York: Dover Publications, 2003.

"Cuna." *Encyclopedia Britannica. https://www.britannica.com/topic/Cuna.*

Darwin, Charles. *On the Origin of Species.* New York: Penguin Books, 1985.

Giroux, Zach. "WWII Gun Mount Resurfaces on Sullivan's Island Beach." *Moultrie News*, Dec. 3, 2018. *News@MoultrieNews.com.*

Hawk, Brandon W. *Apocrypha for Beginners; A Guide to Understanding and Exploring Scriptures Beyond the Bible.* New York: Rockridge Press, 2021.

Healy, Edna. *Wives of Fame - Mary Livingstone, Jenny Marx, Emma Darwin.* London: Sidgwick and Jackson, 1986.

Herbert, Kari. *Polar Wives; The Remarkable Women behind the World's Most Daring Explorers*. Vancouver: Greystone Books, 2012.

Huguenot Society of South Carolina, Founded in 1885. Charleston: Huguenot Society of South Carolina, 2015.

Jahner, Harold. *Aftermath: Life in the Fallout of the Third Reich 1945-1955*. New York: Alfred A. Knopf, 2022.

Josette, Elayi. *The History of Phoenicia*. Columbus, Ga: Lockwood Press, 2018.

Langford, George Shealey. *Langfords in America*. College Park, MD: Langford, 1977.

Langford Land Records. Archives of Land Records and Deeds, Edgefield County Register of Deeds, Edgefield, SC.

Mackenzie, Rob, "David Livingstone - The Truth Behind the Legend," 1999.

Marshall Reservation, Sullivan's Island, vertical files, South Carolina Room, Charleston Country Public Library, Malcolm Hale researcher, July 2023.

Martin, David. *Kilomanjaro*. Harare, Zimbabway: African Publishing Group International, 1999.

McKee, Alexander. *Dresden 1945; The Devil's Tinderbox*. Chicago: Souvenir Press, 1982.

Miklowitz, Gloria D. *Masada: the Last Fortress*. Grand Rapids, MI: Eerdmans Publishing Co., 1998.

"Nazi Death Camps (Treblinka, Solebar and Auschwitz)." *History Magazine*, 24 (2023) no. 2: 42.

Osborne, Milton. *Angkor Wat*. Singapore: Raffles International, Ltd. www.edmbooks.com, 2001.

Oxford, Pete and Bish Renee Oxford. *Galapagos, the Untamed Isles*. No place: Natural Highlights Publishing, 1990.

Patmos: The Holy Island of the Aegean; A Complete Tourist Guide. Perestiri, Attiki, Greece: Editions Micalis Toubis Publications, 1996.

Peckham, J. Brian. *Phoenicia: Episodes and Anecdotes from the Ancient Mediterranean*. Winona Lake, IN: Eisinbrauns Publishing, 2014.

Pollett, Krista. *Sullivan's Island in War Time*. Sullivan's Island, SC: National Park Service, 2023.

Porterfield, Eric S. *Sessions with Galatians; Finding Freedom through Christ.* No place: Smith & Heles Publishing, 1969.

Presnell Records, Huguenot Society of Manakin, Manakin, VA.

Prioleau, Robert Means, Harriott Cheves Leland, and Dianne Watts Ressinger. *Huguenot Footprints: The Journey to America.* Charleston: Huguenot Society of South Carolina, 2010.

Rasheta, Noah. *No-Nonsense Buddhism for Beginners.* San Antonio, TX: Althea Press, 2018.

Ratti, Fabio. *Sicily.* New York: D.K. Publishers, 2000.

Sammut, Felix. *Saint Paul in Malta.* Rabat, Malta: Conventual Franciscans, 2000.

Smith, Charlene. Robben Island (Mayebuye History and Literature Series No. 76) New York: B.H.B. Distribution, 1997.

The Hermitage; A Tour of Halls and Rooms. Istanbul: Alfa Colour Art Publishers, 2007.

Weger, Robert A. *The Swastika: A History.* No place: Trebor Regew & Associates, 1991.

Wolfe, Michael. *The Conversion of Henry IV.* Cambridge, MA: Harvard University Press, 1993.

Wright, Tom. *Paul for Everyone: The Prison Letters.* London: Society for Promoting Christian Knowledge, 2002.